Praise for *The Four Noble Truths of Love*

"Susan Piver brings together decades of wisdom and experience from both her Buddhist practice and her relationships. This book is direct, insightful and honest to its core. Using the lens of the Buddha's noble truths and the path of liberation, Susan presents a practical road map that can be accessed by anyone. I don't think a book quite like this has been written before. She is definitely a wise guide on what it truly means to love altogether and how compassion and insight can be mined from the ups and downs of everyday life and every connection. Susan presents the biggest view possible on what love can be—it's quite an invitation."

JOSH BARAN, author of *The Tao of Now: Daily Wisdom from Mystics, Sages, Poets, and Saints*

"*The Four Noble Truths of Love* is like the book baby of the Buddha and Oprah Winfrey. It pulls no punches in the best of ways. Chock-full of relationship a-ha moments, it made me reflect not just on my marriage and how to keep deepening into it, but also on every loving relationship in my life. This wisdom may be thousands of years old, but Piver's ability to convey it with grace, humor, humility, and profound relevance to modern life is a true gift. Get it, read it, live it!"

JONATHAN FIELDS, founder of Good Life Project

"Susan Piver consistently offers what so many of us seek: A generous, caring, loving teacher, someone with an open heart and a clear mind, eager to help us find our own way forward."

SETH GODIN, author of *Linchpin*

"If you've ever felt that secret shame of not loving well or not managing to embody that perfect detached modern-day Buddha you know you're supposed to be, this is not only your book, it is your salvation. Susan's message, voice, and real world guidance show you the way out of the illusions and traps of relationship and into a level of freedom that is at once both profound and practical."

CHRISTINE KANE, founder and CEO of Uplevel You

"Susan Piver does far more than tell us how the Four Noble Truths apply to love, she lives that application with great depth and honesty, and lets us come along for the ride. Give your heart—and your capacity to do the toughest spiritual work of all, be in relationship—a gorgeous boost with this brilliant guide."

JENNIFER LOUDEN, author of *The Woman's Comfort Book* and *The Life Organizer*

"This is the only book you need for your romantic relationship—it's just that good. Honest, wise, and raw, Susan will show you the four truths you need to actually make your relationship last."

LODRO RINZLER, author of *Love Hurts: Buddhist Advice for the Heartbroken*

"Susan has combined three threads to give us a beautiful tapestry of spiritually conscious love: We find a clear and in-depth view of Buddhism. We see how it offers a path to intimate love. Susan uses her own relationship as an example of how it all comes together. This is a stand-out book for enriching love and closeness along the spiritual path."

DAVID RICHO, author of *How to Be an Adult in Relationships: The Five Keys to Mindful Loving*

"Clear and heart-warming, this book is a guide to living relationships completely, with all their pleasures and otherwise. Susan Piver brought the four noble truths to life in her own marriage, and here shares the fullness of that experience. A wonderful read."

SHARON SALZBERG, author of *Real Love: The Art of Mindful Connection*

The Four Noble Truths of Love

SUSAN PIVER

THE FOUR NOBLE TRUTHS OF LOVE

BUDDHIST WISDOM *for* MODERN RELATIONSHIPS

© 2018 The Open Heart Project / Susan Piver

All rights reserved. No part of this book may be reproduced, stored in a retrieval system or transmitted, in any form or by any means, without the prior written consent of the publisher, except in the case of brief quotations, embodied in reviews and articles.

Lionheart Press, Somerville, MA, USA
susanpiver.com/open-heart-project

ISBN 978-1-7322776-0-1 (paperback)
ISBN 978-1-7322776-1-8 (ebook)

Permission to reprint a lyric from "Rain Just Falls" kindly granted by its author, David Halley.

Some of this material first appeared in articles written for *Lion's Roar* magazine. The author thanks them for their kind permission to reprint.

www.lionsroar.com

Every reasonable effort has been made to contact the copyright holders for work reproduced in this book.

Produced in consultation with Page Two
www.pagetwostrategies.com
Cover and interior design by Taysia Louie
Cover illustration courtesy iStock
Printed and bound in the United States of America

18 19 20 21 22 5 4 3 2 1

Also by Susan Piver

How Not to Be Afraid of Your Own Life

The Wisdom of a Broken Heart

Start Here Now: An Open-Hearted Guide to the Path and Practice of Meditation

For Duncan, who taught me how to stay, and for the Open Heart Project: I wrote this for you.

CONTENTS

The only true elegance is vulnerability.

CHÖGYAM TRUNGPA

INTRODUCTION

How I Discovered the Four Noble Truths of Love

SOME TIME AGO, my husband, Duncan, and I were locked in a state of ongoing disagreement. This disagreement had no center, theme, object, or subject. It was more like a demonic presence. Whatever we discussed gave rise to conflict, whether it was about what time to leave for the movies, if the dishes in the dishwasher were clean or dirty, which bank to use, or if we belonged together as a couple. Once we even argued about what time it was. Even a question as simple as "Where do you want to eat dinner?" could provoke talk of divorce.

(True story: When I posed this question one night, we were driving on a country road and, for some reason, we exploded at each other. I made him pull over and let me out of the car… in France. I had no idea where we were. I didn't care—I just wanted out. I walked into a field until I got scared and went back to the car, arms folded.)

When we were to go somewhere, we disagreed about what we would do once we arrived. When someone said something to us, we disagreed about what it meant. When we attempted to discuss our relationship woes, we disagreed about how to do so, where to lay blame, and how to resolve them. This went on not for days or weeks, but for months. We tried many solutions: talking, not talking, making love, avoiding each other, yelling, ignoring, and, finally, at least for me, just sobbing. Nothing worked. Every interaction ended with anger, hurt feelings, or numbness. I felt so lonely, and I am sure he did too. What was going on? There was nothing to argue about, yet everything provoked conflict. It was dreadful, terrifying. We were afraid to go near each other.

I was ready to admit defeat. I thought, *I have no idea where to begin fixing this*. Then a voice whispered to me: *Begin at the beginning*. (Why are these voices always so simple and correct? And why don't they pipe up earlier?) It continued: *At the beginning are four noble truths. They are:*

Life is suffering (because everything changes).
Grasping is the cause of suffering.
It is possible to stop suffering.
There is a path for doing so.

As a twenty-years-plus student of Buddhism, these words meant something to me. What *would* the dharma say about my dilemma, I wondered. Why had I never thought to examine this question in relation to my relationship? After all, my Buddhist practice and study had been an unfailing guide for two decades in all other areas of my life.

But could these ancient truths be applied to my search for a lasting relationship? I was doubtful. Since the majority of great teachers lived in monasteries or caves and turned their backs on the things of this world so that they could fully embrace the spiritual path through prayer, devotion, and unconventionality, I had subtly imagined that their teachings would not be relevant to my modern love-life problems. I mean, they lived in monasteries, not apartments. They meditated in forests, not on the subway. They had no spouses, possessions, jobs, or bank accounts. Yes, they taught deeply, brilliantly, piercingly about love and the sacred world of emotions, but until this moment I had never thought to apply these teachings to twenty-first-century love affairs, relationships, and heartbreak. When I did, I found a source of profound illumination that enabled me to work with my relationship problems—not to resolve them and tie them up with neat bows, but as an unerring road map back to love and intimacy. Best of all, this road map was not useful just to me, but to my husband as well, even though he is not a Buddhist practitioner. No particular beliefs, dogmas, or practices were needed to mine this wisdom.

To apply a Buddhist viewpoint to relationships is eye-opening. It points to a radically different worldview, one that runs counter to the spirit of much of the conventional advice we receive. It prioritizes unending curiosity over conclusiveness in such a way that conclusions are never arrived at while openness of heart and of mind continue to expand. It posits having no agenda as a path to attainment. It suggests that the solution to problems in the outer world are solved by making changes within and that problems within are solved by dissolving the boundary between self and other. To examine these views carefully is to turn ourselves upside down over and over and, rather than finding explanations by stabilizing in the upside-down, we find what we seek in the turning itself.

As far as I know, this work on relationships is the first written by a Western Buddhist teacher who is also a wife. I humbly hold the intention to bring Buddhist teachings of the highest sort out of the monastery, out of cultural trappings, and into our living rooms, out on our grocery store runs, to our arguments over money, and to what it means to love altogether. The limits I face in sharing this with you are my personal limits as a student and a teacher. On one hand, I am quite daunted because I know my own spiritual puniness, but on the other, my impediments keep me just confused enough to continually question and vet my own notions. Rather than speaking to you from the remove of a perfected relationship, I come to you from deep in the middle of the fray myself but armed with the extraordinary trick bag that comes from two decades of serious Buddhist practice and study. I hope that you will find my offering to you to be both helpful and honest. I hope that you will benefit from my clarity and confusion equally.

The first part of this book sets out the ground of our investigation. We will explore the Four Noble Truths as taught by the Buddha more than 2,500 years ago. Then we will apply them to relationships as the Four Noble Truths of Love.

Following this is an examination of each truth through a combination of reflections on ancient teachings and personal essays from my own life on what it is like to apply these teachings in my own relationship. We will look at principles and practices for actually implementing the Four Noble Truths of Love, which is far more meaningful than considering their logic. It is one thing to read an instruction manual, but it is another to apply what you have learned in real time. Whether in bed or battle, the manual is always left behind, and anyway, as boxer Mike Tyson once said, "Everyone has a plan till they get punched in the face." The point here is that studying the rules of engagement may be useful, but only up to a point. Books eventually go back on the shelf, and what really matters is what you are capable of when love arises from nowhere, hearts are shattered, and the best-laid plans dissolve.

Finally, I will share three practices with you that help you to go beyond simply understanding the Four Noble Truths. They will actually change the way your heart works to make it more open, flexible, and strong because these practices have the power to deepen compassion, wisdom, and confidence in love itself.

The first practice is the all-important practice of mindfulness-awareness meditation, which creates a strong foundation for everything you will read in this work. It is essential.

The second practice is *maitri* (lovingkindness) meditation in two forms: first, the traditional and then a way that is specific to couples. This practice actually teaches you about love that extends beyond (but still includes) what you may feel on any given day.

In the third practice, I will offer you a way to converse with each other as a spiritual practice. Rather than sitting alone and silently working with your mind, this technique puts you in direct contact with each other. It is a practice for you to do together.

Though these practices (the first two in particular) are fundamental to Buddhism, I am not suggesting that you and your partner should become Buddhists, adopt certain beliefs, or become spiritual acolytes. Rather, I offer them as a way to work with your thoughts and feelings in every relationship you have. Without such a way, you will be at the mercy of preconceived notions, childhood woundings, outdated judgments, and bad habits—all of which you will project onto others who are also struggling with the contents of their own mind. When this happens, our neuroses are having the real relationship, not our hearts.

Everything in this book is designed to point you over and over to your inherent goodness and your indestructible capacity to love. You will find encouragement to take the biggest view possible of love, not as a protected hiding place but as a path of courage and openness that leads to true joy.

On Love Affairs and Relationships

Though this work is entitled *The Four Noble Truths of Love*, I want to point out that it may be more applicable to relationships than to love affairs. *What is the difference?* you may ask. If you are from France, you may know what

I am talking about, but for the rest of us, let me explain it this way:

Love affairs and relationships are not the same thing.

No one really tells us this.

When the subject of committing to a relationship—marriage—came up between my husband and me, I went into a panic. Marriage? Why would I do that to someone I loved? Straight up, most of the couples I have ever known seem trapped, unhappy, or done with each other. It rarely seems to work out. Even the most glorious of love affairs can founder on the shore of relationship. Why is it so difficult to transition from one to the other?

From the time I was a child, I was very uncomfortable around most adult couples. I could tell they didn't really like each other. They mocked each other in big and small ways. They ignored each other. One would talk and the other would roll their eyes. Slights, insults, and heavy-heartedness abounded. The longer a couple were together, it seemed, the less they seemed to like each other. How could they bear it? I swore to myself a million times, *I will never be one of those people.*

So when my wonderful boyfriend asked me to marry him, my first thought was, *I will never be one of those people.* But how does one avoid this? Certainly, all the cranky couples had, conceivably, once been as in love as we were. Why should we be any different? When I tried to imagine what might have happened, I had a realization out of the blue (that voice again...): *Just because you love someone does not mean you will love your life together.*

What?! No one had ever said anything about this. Once two people fall in love, every movie, song, and book fades to black. All their problems, it is intimated, are solved. But falling in love and having a relationship are simply two different things. We may believe that love affairs should turn into relationships and relationships should remain love affairs, but the truth is, this is rare.

Most relationships begin as a love affair. That is fantastic, amazing—totally worth pining for, celebrating, appreciating, enjoying, and embracing. Love is real. Falling in love is real. Transcendent romance is... well, it's everything. When I fell in love with Duncan it was like suddenly waking up on a different planet. I was transported to a god realm of beauty, desire, warmth, joy, and satisfaction. Everything made me happy, even the things that made me sad, because everything was meaningful.

I enjoyed my visit to that planet very much. I think of it often. Unfortunately, we cannot live there. We exist in a more human realm. No matter how deep our longing to return to the god planet, longing will not transport us there; auspicious coincidence is the sole means of transport. That almost every relationship book in the world tries to explain how to get there (by making lists and holding visions) is crazy. It is like me writing a book telling rain how to fall. It just doesn't work that way. "Rain don't fall for the flowers, if it's falling. Rain just falls," wrote Texas singer-songwriter David Halley.

When most of us say we are looking for love, what we really mean is we are looking for a ride to Planet Awesome. I hope you will take that ride, many, many times, as often as you like. Nonetheless, you will always, always have to return here. Love affairs happen beyond the mist. Relationships happen on earth.

When our relationships become less than effortless, we may think that we have done something wrong, that we have unhealed childhood wounds, or that our partner has issues they really, really need to resolve. All of this is probably true, but none of it is indicative of a problem. The real problem is that we may have confused love affairs with relationships. Both are indeed potent, but they are not the same. It's when we stop trying to see a relationship as only an extended love affair that we gain access to its unique and often undercelebrated powers: of warmth; of solace; of protection; of friendship, a connection that slows and deepens until it subsumes both hearts and blurs the lines between you, me, and us. That is when it gets very interesting. Anyone can fall in love. But this is just an invitation to the world's most complex and unusual party: the party of two.

Your Critical Intelligence Is Crucial

I want to be very clear that the Four Noble Truths of Love are my invention. The Buddha never taught them, and you will find them in none of the essential texts. As such, it is of utmost importance to examine them very carefully, with your own intelligence as the primary guide.

This admonishment, by the way, is always relevant. Whether teachings are attributed to Buddhas, saints, gurus, unseen beings, your parents, psychologists, journalists, liberals, conservatives, or Susan Piver, you must question them until you are satisfied that they are true. Intelligent doubt is one of your dearest friends, especially in those areas where we feel particularly confused and afraid and therefore the most anxious for blueprints. A blueprint may be a realistic option if you're renovating a garage or installing software, but when it comes to, say, love, death, or sex, there is no such thing. Therefore, though I will do my best to be clear, it is on you to do the work of hearing accurately, contemplating thoroughly, and, finally, testing what you have learned against your actual experience. Otherwise, this will all remain conceptual nonsense that is more likely to confuse than illuminate. What you find to be true is now your wisdom. You own it. What you cannot corroborate, feel free to leave behind.

I am very excited to think about the writings and teachings that are to come in my lifetime and beyond on the topic of ancient Buddhist wisdom applied to modern relationships. We stand on the precipice of an entirely new—and completely accessible—way of understanding how our hearts work so that we may offer them more fully, gracefully, and genuinely to each other. (I wish I could live for another five hundred years to see how it all unfolds.) I hope that this book will contribute to the burgeoning dialogue.

A quick note on gender pronouns: As I was writing this work, I experimented with everything I could think of to express no gender or sexual orientation preference between straight, gay, trans, bisexual, binary, nonbinary, and so on. I consulted Google, friends, and a professor of Women and Gender Studies. I experimented with "he or she," "he and/or she," "them." I even made up my own glyph, "he +/–/= she," to indicate all the possible preferences. In the end, I simply decided to go with "he or she" or "they." This is not meant to exclude or offend anyone but was a choice made in the name of simplicity.

I want also to call attention to the fact that I am a white woman in a relationship with a white man. As such, I come from a place of white privilege and racial biases that I am working to acknowledge, expose, and liberate so that I may love, lead, and support others to heal the palpable divide. There may be pieces of this work that come across as non-inclusive and tone deaf when it comes to race. I apologize for my lack of insight. It is very much a work in progress. If you, dear reader, would be kind enough to point out my unobserved inner biases, I would be in your debt. You can reach me via my website.

Finally, a caveat. What I am about to share with you is derived from my years as a student (and, later, a teacher) of Buddhism. I have had the astounding good fortune to study with truly great masters who, with more generosity than I ever dreamed possible, gave teachings of the most profound sort to this student whose mind is too thick to comprehend them fully. As I endeavor to share it all with you, it is quite possible that I will misrepresent something. If so, this is entirely my fault and no reflection whatsoever on the elegance and realization of my beloved teachers.

I wish you many blessings on this journey. My heart goes with you.

The Four Noble Truths of Buddhism

The Four Noble Truths of Buddhism are the very first teachings the Buddha gave upon attaining enlightenment, and the entire Buddhist path is based on them. Countless words have been written on each of these four, and you could spend a lifetime in contemplation of just one of them.

The Buddha (which means "awakened one") arrived at these truths after many years of searching. Given his circumstances, it is somewhat miraculous that he attempted this search at all. Siddhartha Guatama (his given name) was born a prince and lived a protected life of luxury. Under orders from his father, the king, Siddhartha was not to be deprived of anything. He was to be given whatever might bring him pleasure and shielded from anything that could deprive him of it. However, no matter how determined you are or how fortunate your circumstances, it is impossible to escape difficulty, and during his early life, he had experiences that led him to believe that all was not perfect. One day, he was being driven by his charioteer, Chandaka. Along the way, they passed an elderly person. Buddha had never seen an old person before and asked Chandaka what was wrong with the man. Chandaka replied, "He is old." Then they passed by someone who was coughing and weak. Again, the Buddha was confused. "That is a sick person," said Chandaka. Finally, they encountered a funeral. When Buddha asked what this was about, Chandaka explained that people die and the mourners were carrying a corpse.

Buddha was thrown into a state of confusion and longing, much as you or I would be if we had never seen old age, sickness, or death. To have all three sprung on him suddenly caused great discomfort and greater inspiration. *I must solve these problems*, thought Buddha. *It cannot be that all of us are at the mercy of old age, sickness, and death. This makes no sense.* (Perhaps you, too, have had such thoughts.) Against the wishes of his father, Buddha left his life of luxury and ease to discover the truth of existence and find answers to such questions as "What is the point?" "How can we escape suffering?" "Is there a deeper meaning?" and so on. (Perhaps you, too, have asked such questions.) He abandoned what most of us strive for—wealth, comfort, and unceasing amusements—in order to discover the true nature of reality and, in so doing, transcend the cycle of suffering for himself and others. He experimented with all of the methods of his day, some of which are not terribly foreign to us: various yogic disciplines, fasting, and other forms of asceticism. Though he learned something from each of them, none liberated him from suffering. Finally, one day he sat underneath a tree with the intention of remaining there, completely still, until realization dawned... which it did. (This took either seven or forty-nine days, depending on your source.)

When he returned to his fellow seekers, they saw that he had attained what they were all seeking: liberation from suffering. When they asked him about his radiant state, he said that, upon fully waking up to reality, he had found four things to be true:

The truth of suffering. This does not mean that life sucks, but that everything changes and there is actually nothing to hold on to. This is very painful. We're always trying to establish our ground, to build something stable and steady. And we can't, at least not for very long. Everything that arises eventually dissolves: our bodies, homes, relationships, possessions, accomplishments—there is nothing whatsoever that we can hold on to. This causes a lot of stress. It is extremely hard to accept that there are no exceptions to the truth of impermanence.

The cause of suffering. It is not the dissolution of who and what we love that causes suffering, it is trying to hold on anyway. Grasping creates suffering. If we did not try to hold on, if we were not continually engaged in a battle with impermanence, if we accepted that whatever causes joy, sorrow, security, insecurity, pain, or boredom cannot last, we would not suffer.

The cessation of suffering. Having identified the cause of suffering, we now know that it is possible to stop suffering. "It hurts when I go like this," said every child. "Don't go like this," said every parent. In other words, stop grasping.

The path to no suffering. There is a Noble Eightfold Path that, when followed, will liberate you. The eight steps are: Right View, Right Intention, Right Speech, Right Action, Right Effort, Right Livelihood, Right Mindfulness, and Right Concentration. (We will explore these eight in a later chapter.)

To apply these four truths to everyday life means to accept that things won't ever quite work out (at least not in any conventional sense); that when you hold on to anything too tightly (even the idea of not holding on to anything too tightly), it backfires; that it is all workable; and, finally, that there is a step-by-step explanation for how to do so, via practices, insights, devotion, and so on.

The Four Noble Truths of Love

When I was in the deepest part of my suffering over my relationship problems, it was these four truths that spontaneously came to mind. At first, as mentioned, I was stymied about how to apply them to my love life. Then I saw that there was an underlying logic and progression to the Four Noble Truths: first, a statement of the problem; second, identification of the cause; third, a solution; fourth, how to apply the solution.

Given this, what came to me is the following, which I call the Four Noble Truths of Love. They are:

Relationships never stabilize. When you solve one problem, another arises. There is actually no way to finally get comfortable. They are constantly in flux because relationships are alive.

Expecting relationships to be stable is what makes them unstable. The second truth, the cause of suffering, is that we expect them to stabilize anyway. We are always trying to get rid of the problems in our relationships. This is only human. However, expecting that, upon doing so, you will finally be happy can cause a lot of confusion. Though there may be moments or periods of vast happiness and comfort, they will always fade, no matter how hard we try, how many relationship books we read, or how many therapy visits we make. Thinking that a relationship will finally come to rest in a peaceful place is actually what makes it uncomfortable. When that expectation is softened, an enormous space opens up.

Meeting the instability together is love. Rather than trying to resolve the discomfort of instability, a relationship is about riding the never-ending waves of connection, distance, desire, dullness, and joy, together. In so doing, you find that there is an ever-present invitation to deepen intimacy, whether you agree or disagree, are delighted or confounded by each other.

The path to liberation. Finally, there are steps we can take to go beyond disconnection and disagreement to love each other more deeply. In this way, love turns from a transactional experiment to a way of becoming more fully alive, human, and powerful.

Let's look at each truth in turn.

I

TRUTH #1

Relationships Never Stabilize

TO ME, MY husband has an awful way of fighting. When it comes to arguing, I am very much a rules-of-engagement person. He is more of a street fighter who reacts in the moment. He loses his temper. He gets red in the face. He brings up unrelated issues. He won't let go.

This is a serious problem. The way he fights is not right; there is no question; I do not care what anyone says. As the years have gone by, I have veered from *Okay, we can work with this* to *No way—I will not work with this, and if it happens again, I am out.* When he loses his temper, it is very, very, very unpleasant for me. Luckily, over the years, he has worked hard on this, and the issue is nowhere near what it was when we were first together. It has been painful for him to address it. It has been painful for me, too.

At some point in most long-term relationships, discomfort such as this can reach epic proportions and may actually cause the relationship to end. One never knows.

But the discomfort of instability isn't limited to long-standing interpersonal issues. Whether you're on a blind date, worrying if you'll like each other, or have been married for twenty years groaning yet again, "Why are you doing that thing that I've asked you eleventy billion times not to do?" this discomfort is there.

Getting together with someone for the first time is unsettling. What if your date likes you? What if they don't? Even before the first meeting, you may think about past relationships and how they hurt you, make lists of warning signs to watch for, consult with friends about whether or not you remain desirable. Before you have even met this person, there is so much hope and so much fear that it can be unbearable.

Falling in love has its own special instability. Though it is truly blissful, instability here looks like an inability to pay attention to anything or anyone else. One is subject to great, heaving waves of emotion, some of which are quite beautiful while others are terrifying. There is a sense of living on the very edge of your sense perceptions, emotional capacity, and mental stability. You could spend a sleepless night worrying about the way your beloved looked at you—*What did that expression mean?* The slightest disconnect is so painful. Each meeting is a revelation. Every moment

feels very alive (because it is) but also quite inte
could spin out at any moment.

Should you settle into an ongoing relationship, it is inevitable that you will discover things that you do not like about each other. The magic of new love begins to settle into something more conventional. (Some people are heartbroken by this, while others are relieved.)

I remember after one night of ecstatic lovemaking, I came downstairs to find my boyfriend in the kitchen, removing all the dishes I had placed in the dishwasher in order to replace them in the "correct" manner. There was something about the juxtaposition of transcendent love against what I viewed as bourgeois persnicketiness that made my heart sink. How did my wild lover turn into this guy who has opinions about the dishwasher? Does this mean I have to learn a new way of loading the machine? What if I don't want to? What else am I going to have to change about myself?

It is uncomfortable to imagine that in order to create a happy household, we will have to pay attention to such minute details. But we do. Tiny power struggles begin to emerge and, honestly, from my observation it is these utterly inconsequential disagreements that end up eroding a perfectly good relationship. That these things accrue is pretty ridiculous, but nonetheless true.

Why this happens at all is of great interest. When we fall in love, we are possessed by such bigness of heart and mind. We see only the highest and deepest meaning of our life. Everyday hassles are seen as minor irritants, easily metabolized, not relevant when one has just discovered a capacity for joy, pleasure, and doubtlessness.

However…

It would seem that as capable as you are of love, you also possess tremendous self-doubt. Very few individuals are naturally convinced of their inherent worthiness. (In fact, in Buddhist thought, to possess such conviction is considered a corollary of full enlightenment.) It's more likely that we are caught in cycles of self-denigration and self-aggrandizement, both of which are forms of aggression. We are so hard on ourselves, so unremittingly unkind in the way we consider ourselves. The opposite, insisting that we are in fact awesome, is simply the flip side of that thought pattern.

When it comes to love, unkindness to self begins to mix with the relationship. As you become emotionally intertwined, the energetic space between you starts to close up. As it tightens, your ability to see your partner as separate from your own mindstream diminishes. The closer you get, the less able you are to actually see each other. What happens at this point is that because you cannot discern who is who, you begin to treat your beloved the way you treat your own mind. The kindness or unkindness you extend toward them is a reflection of the way you treat yourself. Generosity of spirit, so powerful in the early stages of a relationship, begins to contract.

Here, "generosity" is defined as a gesture rooted in recognition of your store of unending riches that can never be depleted. Under such circumstances, to give is easy, obvious, and free. It is beneficent. Discomforts are more easily resolved. Without such certainty, however, being generous to others is quite difficult. You are easily slighted. Your "territory" may be encroached upon by another's needs, opinions, and habitual ways of inhabiting space. For example, I have a low tolerance for noise, especially in the morning when I'm trying to segue noiselessly into my morning routine. My husband likes to start his day by Googling around for video footage of musicians he loves. If you don't love music in the morning and suddenly find your home echoing with Yellowman at Reggae Sunsplash 1982, you might become snappish even though you also happen to love Yellowman... and your husband. What was adorable in the first month may become irritating after the first decade, for no other reason than that you (and me and everyone else) exist in a very ordinary state that Buddhists call "all-pervasive suffering." (Like northern Indigenous peoples are said to have for snow, Buddhists have a thousand names for suffering.) This is the kind of suffering that you cannot quite point to as caused by this or that but that haunts your every experience with hope that you will finally get what you want or fear that you won't. It is a kind of free-floating anxiety that we humans live with. The closer we become with another, the more our unnameable and persistent states of agitation mingle. Naturally, the anxiety can be detonated at any time, whether by music that is too loud, dishes that are put away wrong, or the nth time he or she is twenty minutes late for everything.

At one point in our early marriage, we went to a marriage counselor for help figuring out why each found the other so annoying. Luckily, this man was a genius and we owe him an unending debt of gratitude. (Shout out to Rich Borofsky!) Of the many memorable things he taught us, one was this: "Relationships are full of irritation." It's true! There is something about continual proximity to another person that is irritating. They put their coat on the chair instead of hanging it up. They buy the wrong kind of pasta at the market. They lose their keys after you have told them again and again to put them in the same place every time they come home. I know these things are truly first-world ridiculous but no "I will rise above this pettiness" mindset is going to save you from this particular form of discomfort. The truth is, we are sensitive and small-minded and very easily hurt. That's okay. We're only human.

And of course, there is the deeper issue of encountering the same emotional or psychological disconnects over years, decades, forever—and despairing of ever changing each other. This is *extremely* destabilizing. On some days, the instability feels like, "Oh well, that's just the way she is and I love her anyway even though it hurts me," while on others it feels like the straw that breaks the camel's back and causes you to consider separation.

So whether you have not even met your date yet or are about to rehash the same argument with your life partner, relationships are unstable.

I actually find this kind of heartening. Instead of constantly working to get comfortable in my relationship and feeling that something is wrong because I can't ever quite get there, I can relate with the instability as a strange invitation to remain awake in love. So if you were ever thinking, "When am I ever going to get comfortable in this relationship?" I invite you to consider that the answer might be "Never."

I've come to think that the most deeply loving gesture I can make within my relationship is to tolerate my own discomfort; to recognize my feelings and leave the story behind; to cease and desist from threatening my husband with consequences should he fail to be the person I need him to be rather than the person he is.

There is something magical—yes, magical—about this discomfort. You are right there, never quite in your comfort zone. There is no possibility of falling asleep. You are always a tiny bit on the edge, as if you are trying something new for the very first time. When it comes to love, this is not such a bad approach. Brilliance and inspiration and everything fresh are discovered on this edge, including how to open your heart beyond what you ever thought possible.

This is the noble experiment of love.

BIG HONKING EXCEPTION TO EVERYTHING I JUST SAID—YOU MUST READ THIS:

There are some sources of instability that are NOT OKAY. The ideas in this book are meant to apply to ordinary relationship issues that may fall anywhere along the spectrum from bothersome (*Why do you always show up late/interrupt me/drive too slow?*) to shocking (*You cheated on me/lied about your finances/told me your sexual orientation was this when it was really that*). Certain problems can be truly excruciating and make you feel that your life is falling apart... and it may be. However, while some sources of instability feel like unremitting betrayals, they are not necessarily indications of physical, mental, or emotional abuse. When I suggest that tolerating instability is a gateway to intimacy, **I am not including instability due to physical abuse or addiction, or emotional abuses such as stonewalling or being constantly insulted or demeaned.** These things are in a different category, and no one should feel that they ought to tolerate problems that require professional help and are not only out of their control, but may be out of their partner's control as well. *Promise me you will not forget this.*

Riding Instability

> *The bad news is, you're falling through the air, nothing to hang on to, no parachute. The good news is, there is no ground.*
>
> CHÖGYAM TRUNGPA

To say yes to love is to say yes to the unfolding, impenetrable arc of uncertainty. I had thought that finding love was an endpoint, that some kind of search was over and I would find home. Finally, I would be able to get comfortable. We would leap over the threshold together into whatever we imagined our ideal cottage to be. But really we stepped through a looking glass. No matter how hard we try, how crazy in love we are, or how skillfully we plan our life together, there is complete uncertainty about what our connection will feel like from day to day. I can give all the love I have (with great joy) and get back a blank stare. I can wake up as my crankiest, most sullen and narcissistic self, roll over, and greet the face of unconditional acceptance. Or not. It's like the weather. You could read the signs and guess about atmospheric conditions, but really, any type of front could blow through on any given day—and, like listening to a meteorologist explain why it's going to rain, I think, "Who cares why? I just want to know what to wear today."

We can't actually promise each other anything. The relationship never stabilizes, ever. This is the way it works. I have no idea why.

This isn't to say that we should give up on trying to solve our problems. It's not that you should just stay in any relationship no matter what (see previous caveat), but if you find yourself thinking, *If only we could solve this one problem, everything will be fine* or *My partner has got to stop doing _____ and then I'll feel great about us*, I invite you to reconsider. Yes, work on your problems. Don't give up unless absolutely necessary. But working on problems is not the problem here. Expecting that happiness will come from solving them is.

Sometimes I look at Duncan and cry because I cannot believe that someday we're going to have to say goodbye to each other. I love him so much. I cannot bear the thought that one of us will die first and the other will be alone. It breaks my heart into a billion pieces and I find the whole situation unbearably precious, so much so that I think I may pass out. Other times we have some kind of argument and I behold him with absolute coldness. I don't care about him at all; I just want him to leave me alone. Yet other times, I look at him and think, *Who the hell are you? I have no idea. You are a total stranger to me.* And then I feel very lonely.

This keeps happening. We cycle continuously between *You are my everything*, *I can't stand to be around you*, *Have we met?* and everything in between. At first, I was very disturbed by this. But now, after some years, I kind of go, *Oh well, that's how it is.* It's never going to be predictable.

Naturally, when you are thinking of making a commitment to a relationship, you do so with the thought, *Oh, this is going to make me happy*. Of course! I hope that every relationship you ever have will make you happy, and I want my own relationship to make me happy, but I've come to the conclusion that that is not its primary job. What, then, is?

It seems to be about opening further, further, and further still without quite knowing where it is all heading. In Buddhism, this is called waking up. However, it is not so easy. Three poisons get in the way.

The Three Poisons

Many years ago I was camping in the Sinai desert with my boyfriend. We pitched our tent in a semi-solitary spot but could see other tents dotting the vast golden expanse under the blue, blue sky. Around dusk, we went for a swim in the Red Sea. As we were walking back to our little base camp, we noticed that everyone else was folding up their tents and heading for their cars. Rather than driving off, they appeared to be leaning their seats back to settle in for the night. *Why would they sleep in their cars rather than their tents?* we wondered. We entered ours, lit a small lantern, and sat on our sleeping bags in wet bathing suits to eat the sandwiches we'd brought for dinner. Soon we noticed that the wind was picking up. The tent canvas began to shudder but the lantern remained upright and our little abode seemed to be able to hold its own. We continued eating and talking and marveling at the power of the night—until we noticed that sand had begun to fill the floor of our tent and was rising at an alarming rate. Soon, very soon, maybe even within minutes, we would be drowned in sand. We quickly collapsed our tent, weighted it down with as many rocks as we could find, and headed to our car, sand stinging our skin until it felt like it might draw blood. We could barely see our car, much less drive it out of a sandstorm. We too settled in for the night.

For anyone in a relationship for longer than a minute, this pattern will sound familiar. It's a beautiful day. Everything seems fine. Our home is solid. Signs of trouble may appear, but we either ignore or misinterpret them while we continue to do normal things like talking and eating when suddenly, *suddenly*, SH*T BLOWS UP. While we had been going about our business, minute granules of dissatisfaction were seeping into the walls, piling up imperceptibly, taking us utterly by surprise, threatening, out of nowhere, to tank the whole situation.

In this sense, the insurmountable problems we encounter may actually be connected to the devilishly small details of everyday life. Sure, some relationships suffer grievous harm from betrayals, abuse, and addiction. These are most certainly not small issues. They are devastating. However, they are also fairly clear, as opposed to the general sense of malaise, annoyance, and distance that may arise over time. When you are faced with a big, definable problem, you can consult friends, experts, and organizations. When you are in the sandstorm, there is really no one to talk to because there is nothing to talk *about*. The problem is impossible to pinpoint. Everything seems fine . . . until it doesn't. Then we scramble for an explanation and often settle on something that is only true on the surface. The truth is, no single grain of sand is to blame; however, collectively, they form a massive problem, made more complicated by the fact that you can't really point to any one grain as meaning anything worth considering. We may start to pick issues out of thin air. *You are a slob. You never listen to me. Your friends are terrible. Our home sucks and I want to move.* Okay. Maybe all of these things are true. But, I posit, none of them are the true source of the disconnect. Rather, a host of small slights have consolidated themselves into a mass.

Understandably, we become frustrated because there seems to be nothing to attack. In response and out of an inability to tolerate the discomfort, we may default to what in Buddhism are called "the three poisons," or three unhelpful responses to feeling out of control. One of these is probably your poison of choice and one, usually a different one, may be your partner's.

Passion

The first poison is grasping, sometimes also called passion. You become emotionally overwhelmed and insist on reassurance that everything will be okay. You may become terrified that your partner will leave or swear that *now* you will finally become the partner they desire. You are in a desperate search for good news and everything you encounter is either proof that what you fear is imminent or that it is not. You settle on solutions quickly and attempt to apply them on the spot. Nothing has time to unfold or develop. The blame game takes over, and whether it is aimed at yourself or your partner, the mind shrinks into a very tiny knot. It is extremely claustrophobic. This does not help anyone, least of all yourself.

A note on passion: It is tricky. Many Buddhist practitioners will point to it as the primary problem, the root cause of suffering as expressed in the Second Noble Truth: *Grasping creates suffering.* It's true. In many ways, the entire Buddhadharma is based on the path of nonattachment and non-grasping. But how is it possible to reconcile this with the glorious experience of falling love, the nourishing delight of finding home with another precious being, or the gut-wrenching, no-one-could-ever-prepare-you-for-it shock of a broken heart? All of these speak to a kind of "attachment." Does this mean they are a priori wrong? And if you were to rid yourself of all attachments, would you also find yourself unable to celebrate love or mourn its loss?

Let's begin by taking the sting out of the word "attachment." I find that it's a word people use when they are angry at you for getting upset about something that they don't think you should be upset about, as in, "Oh, you're so attached," in this judgmental, superior way that really pisses me off. (Hey! Why are you so attached to my nonattachment? Have you ever wondered *that*?)

Of course we are attached.

We're attached to our happiness. We're attached to the people we love. We're attached to our longings. There is nothing wrong with this. Nonattachment does not mean you do not feel the joy and suffering of being human. (I mean, it is possible to be attached to nonattachment.) Rather, it means to recognize that everything—every experience, moment, idea, emotion, and form—will arise, abide, and dissolve. Nonattachment is about staying on the ride, no matter what.

Passion between two people will constantly arise, abide, and dissolve. Though this is a very difficult thing to navigate, I don't think it is a problem. Wishing that you were in a different arc of the cycle, however, can be. It is when we dispense of thinking that "nonattachment" is the conversion of all phenomena into an equal tone that we are truly free from grasping. Rather than being nonplussed by pain or pleasure, sanguine in the face of loss, unimpressed by great joy, we are free to experience it all fully and, when it begins to dissolve, to let go. In this sense, nonattachment does not diminish emotions, it increases them. It does not reduce the sharpness of our sense perceptions, it increases it. It amplifies both pain and pleasure. In Buddhist thought, dancing with passion and letting go is considered a path of warriorship. Passion, then, is both a source of great suffering *and* an opportunity to fully liberate your heart from all constraint. It is an invitation to a super-rich sensory experience of your world. Passion is a fire that makes the whole world more colorful. Just like with an actual fire, it is all in how you handle it.

Aggression

The second poison is called aggression. This is when you aim to destroy whatever you deem to be a problem. You may lash out, punish, demean, or discount what or who you hold accountable. (This only serves to strengthen what you oppose, by the way.)

One form that the poison of aggression may take is as a search for any possible explanation or interpretation that will create of this chaos an orderly narrative. It's very strange how this works. I have seen myself do it time after time. *You act this way because you had a bad day at work/ your parents were mean/you are incapable of love. I act this way because I am misunderstood, and if only you would stop/ start this behavior, we would be okay. This means that. That means this.* It is as if the right storyline would solve the problem. While it is really useful to examine behaviors and learn about underlying motivations, sorrows, and confusions, to pointedly insist on an explanation causes your mind to shrink into a very tiny knot. It is extremely claustrophobic. This does not help anyone, least of all yourself.

Ignorance

The third poison is ignorance. You simply hide. You reach for whatever you can to self-narcotize, whether it is videos, drink, exercise, incessant social media surfing, food, drugs, books, or whatever works to keep you asleep to what you feel. You freeze. You try not to move because any wrong step may bring you face to face with your partner and what you are trying to avoid. Ignorance shrinks our mind into a very tiny knot. It is extremely claustrophobic. This does not help anyone, least of all yourself.

Passion, aggression, and ignorance are the masks worn by fear. There is a fourth option. *It is to meet your fear.* Feel it. Instead of turning away, you open to include it. While the three poisons shrink your mind, this is the only response that expands and softens it. You actually relax *with* what you feel rather than working to disprove, demolish, or hide from it. This creates a kind of space in which you treat the people in your life as more than potential devices to be used for good or for ill; instead you treat them as companions on a journey that is sometimes joyful, sometimes horrifying or dull, but always rich with the possibility for greater intimacy. True fearlessness is the simple willingness to open your heart. Bravery is not about quelling opposition. It is about entering the field of relationship, with all its power, chaos, and confusion, to learn how people actually get close to each other, what it means to stretch your capacity to feel, and what causes greater understanding. The gateway is the willingness to feel fear.

This willingness is a consequence of meditation practice. By working with your mind on the cushion, you develop the capacity to work with it off the cushion. This is the entire point of the practice: not to be good at meditating (so what?) but to be good at being yourself. Meditation is not a self-help tactic or a way to be more productive. It is a path of warriorship that enables us to meet our world with steadiness and sanity. (See Appendix A for more on how to meditate.)

Sadness Is Important

The great feminist leader, icon, and powerhouse Gloria Steinem was once asked in an interview if she was depressed over the loss of her husband, who had died only a few years after they married in 2000. She said she was not depressed, she was sad. The journalist asked what the difference was. "In depression, you care about nothing. In sadness, you care about everything," she replied. In other words, when you are depressed, nothing has any meaning. The world is cold and closed. Nothing can touch you. When you are sad, it comes alive. You feel your own feelings more intensely, but you also feel the feelings of others more piercingly. Everything touches you. Depression shuts you down; sadness opens a channel.

One way to change your relationship to love and find the ability to work with instability confidently is not to be bold, resolute, brilliant, or even compassionate. It is to allow for sadness.

When you look at your longing for love and at the disappointments you may have experienced because of it, you may feel sad. If you feel deeper into it, you may discover that your sadness is sweet and tender, shaky and raw. This is good. You are seeing clearly. By developing a tolerance for sadness (rather than reflexively seeking to banish it), you also develop a way to work with the particular forms of discomfort that come with giving and receiving love.

It begins with feeling your own deep wish for love. Don't be scared to do this. You could take a moment and simply admit it. What is it like to do so? When you acknowledge this hunger without shame, you become aware that everyone else is walking around in the exact same state. We want so much to be loved. In fact, you could say that all the craziness in our world began with someone feeling unloved and then being unable or unwilling to face the sadness that resulted. If we felt our sadness, we would actually avoid the three poisons, which, as mentioned, shrink your mind into a tiny, hard peanut. But if you look under the surface of fear, rage, and avoidance, you will find sadness, which is soft, workable, and expansive. The poisons give rise to codependence. Sadness gives rise—spontaneously, naturally, completely—to more tenderness.

Because it is so uncomfortable, we immediately want to turn sadness into what we imagine will hurt less: anger, hopelessness, helplessness. But when the wish to love is rooted in anger, the only result is more confusion. And of course, when we feel hopeless or helpless, we take refuge in non-action, which also creates confusion.

Despair is what happens when you fight sadness. Love is what happens when you don't. It will not feel "good," but it will feel alive. Your heart will remain open. So the key—and this is a big one—is to learn to stabilize your heart in this open state. The practice of meditation is this stabilization. It is so much more than a self-improvement technique: it is a path to love.

2

TRUTH #2

Expecting Relationships to Be Stable Is What Makes Them Unstable

IF YOU SHOP for books about relationships in the self-help section, you will see that roughly 99 percent of them are about how to get love: how to find it, keep it, or make it come back. Very few are about how to give love or be loving. If there are ideas about such things, they are suggested as another way to get more love rather than as an end in themselves. The search for love is portrayed as an elliptical, self-serving endeavor.

In the Buddhist view, the emphasis is shifted. Happiness is not seen as a consequence of getting your needs met. It comes from placing attention on the needs of others, not because you are a goody-goody with no needs, but because the joy of connection, whether to a person, animal, flower, idea, or sensation, is the most profound of all the joys. As my teacher Sakyong Mipham said, "If you want to be happy, think of others. If you want to be unhappy, think of yourself." It was not politeness that made him say so. Yet it is rarely the way we approach love.

To begin, it is helpful to consider that when we say we are looking for love, we may not mean exactly that. Rather, we are looking for safety, a way to get comfortable. "Relationship" is equated not with the crazy, boundary-busting, irritating, empowering, ordinary, extraordinary thing that it really is, but with a protective cocoon. This is understandable. Loving is so vulnerable—maybe the most vulnerable thing you can do—and we want to put as many controls in place as possible to protect our hearts.

However, the moment you try to make love safe, it ceases to be love. There is nothing less safe than love. Love means opening again and again to your beloved, yourself, and your world, and seeing what happens next. You can't know what it will be. Waves of connection are followed by waves of distance. Sunny conditions give way to more sun—or to storms. Storms give way to clear skies. Or not. One simply never knows, and a great deal of presence and bravery is required to face the shifting patterns. The ride cannot be fully evened out; it can only be experienced.

There is no way that you can know how your relationship is going to turn out, regardless of how carefully you prepare, how clear you are about your needs and expectations, and how intently you listen to your partner's wishes.

Yet somehow when we commit to another person, we make and require promises. *I will always love you. I promise to cherish you. Nothing will ever come between us.*

Sometimes you will love each other, and sometimes you will fume with rage.

Sometimes you will cherish your partner, and sometimes you will wish they would, shall we say, disappear.

Something will come between you every single day: work, family, ambitions, depressions, confusions, and different ideas about everything from how much money is enough and which personal values you ought to share to the "right" way to fold laundry.

To enter a relationship for the long term is to enter the space of not knowing. While this is so brave and beautiful, exhilarating even, it is not particularly comfortable.

Romantic Materialism

Tibetan meditation master Chögyam Trungpa defined something called the Three Lords of Materialism. These three lords, known as the Lords of Form, Speech, and Mind, rule physical, psychological, and spiritual materialism. They direct us to acquire certain belongings or qualities with the promise that these will enable us to avoid sorrow and bring us lasting happiness.

The Lord of Form says that there are certain possessions, attainments, and lifestyles that will exempt you from sadness, whether for a moment or for all time. If only you had a house in the right neighborhood, a degree from a specific institute, a certain amount of money in savings, a new iPhone, automobile, job, or hairdo, you would be happy. It's not that these things aren't wonderful. They are! But they will not save you. (Well, maybe the hairdo.)

The Lord of Speech rules the realm of thoughts, beliefs, and philosophies. This Lord assures you that when you can correctly assess your childhood wounds, subscribe to the right ideology, or adhere to the most accurate analysis, you will be safe. It's not that these things aren't wonderful. They are! But they will not save you.

The Lord of Mind is most insidious. He seeks to convince you that meditation or other spiritual practices will exempt you from suffering and give you special status among your fellow humans. If only your meditation was perfect or you could think only "good" thoughts, you would be free from pain. It's not that these things aren't wonderful. They are! But they will not save you.

All three Lords point you down the wrong path. Each seeks to affirm your small mind and conventional view by urging you to create a cocoon that will protect you from suffering. Each would like to obscure your highest wisdom and true nature, which are available only when the cocoon disappears.

I want to take the liberty of suggesting a fourth Lord: the Lord of Romance. So that you may gain entry into a more heavenly realm, rather than directing you to acquire certain possessions, knowledge, or spiritual attainments, this Lord says you can obtain access through falling in love, finding "the one."

He attempts to use our heart connection to another person as a means to escape suffering. He makes the case that relationships will protect us from sorrow, anger, frustration, disappointment, and all manner of physical, emotional, and spiritual loss.

He is in league with the Lord of Form when he tells us to find a wealthy partner so that we can have a nice house and escape financial worry.

He has teamed with the Lord of Speech when we find ourselves caught up in beliefs: that the right one will appear when our childhood wounds are healed; that our partner owes it to us to meet our needs, give us space, eat dinner with us together every night; or any other unchecked assumption about what love ought to be.

And when the Lords of Romantic and Spiritual Materialism get together, hijinks ensue. We might think that our relationship is supposed to provide shelter from every storm, heal our sorrows, fulfill our longings, and create a life of unending happiness. If you are hoping for a relationship that will drop into your lap from heaven, put an end to all of your self-doubt, and snuggle you permanently, you may be running on the fumes of romantic materialism rather than the desire for true love (which is discovered on the spot rather than planned for in advance).

There is nothing wrong with wanting bunches of money, philosophical clarity, spiritual attainment, and the truest of true loves. I hope you will have all of that and more, and that your relationship will give you a life of beauty, heart-to-heart connection, and deep healing on all levels. But if you are looking for safety rather than love, you may be under the sway of materialism rather than true kindheartedness toward self and other.

The Lord of Romantic Materialism takes the wheel every time you think that there is a person out there who was born looking for you just as you were born looking for them, and that, once you find each other, difficulties will cross-dissolve into oblivion. He is present every time you imagine that if only you could visualize him or her clearly, that person would materialize to rescue you. When you subscribe to the belief that healing childhood wounds will remove unseen blockages that prevent your life partner from approaching, you are serving this Lord. He runs on the fumes of magical thinking.

The more important something is to you, the more likely you are to apply magical thinking to it, and when it comes to love, there is no shortage of books and classes that purport to teach you various tricks of mind that will attract what you desire. Please don't waste your time and money. Instead, examine your mind carefully. Analyze the lenses through which you observe the world, and seek to understand the illusions and projections that result. This is of utmost importance. Love will not come to you by imagining what love looks like. Instead of hoping against hope for true love to somehow just show up, hold your heart and mind open. Stop looking for it. Instead, offer it to everyone. In this way, you make a relationship with love itself. The focus is on expanding your heart's capacity rather than on waiting for another to fill it up. By offering your heart in countless big and small ways, you will find that you no longer have to wait for love because you are actually living in it.

The Lord of Romantic Materialism feeds off of fear, distrust, and hopelessness. He enjoys your discomfort and seeks to convince you to focus on disposing of it at any cost by enlisting a fellow human as your foil. However, when you operate from openness and generosity of spirit, he can find no purchase. Much of our discomfort in relationships comes not from normal fights and disconnects, but from paying more attention to these Lords and less to love itself.

No Ultimatums

When we were first thinking of getting married, I lived in one city and my then boyfriend lived in a different city. I loved where I lived! In addition to feeling wonderfully at home in New York City, I had an exciting professional network that helped me to build my business. I did not love Boston, the city he lived in. But he had a young child at that time, in that city. We both had compelling reasons to stay where we were.

This went on for five years, including the first three years of our marriage. (We got married, went on a honeymoon, and then each went back to our own apartment.) At any point, it would have been so easy for one of us to say, "You have to" or "You don't love me unless" or "What does this say about us?" The issue was difficult (and expensive) and seemed to have no resolution. The conversation about it went on and on. And on. We argued. We cried. We were confused. We designed various scenarios. Luckily, there is one thing we did not do, because it would have ended our relationship: at no point did either of us issue an ultimatum.

Instead, somehow—and I really credit him—we simply abided in this very uncomfortable place... for five years. We hung in there until, suddenly, it was resolved. I don't even know how it happened. One day, I woke up and said, "Okay, I'll move there." It just seemed like there was no point in living apart anymore. Yes, we had had the luxury of handling it this way because we could (though barely) afford two households. But at some point, the expense and chaos of two households became untenable. And there is no card that trumps the child card. So after five years, I realized in a split second that I had to move there. And I did. It was not (and it still is not) easy to live in a locale I am not fond of, but when I could do it for us rather than for him, it seemed like a gesture of love rather than defeat.

The Projector

We each have some pretty distinct ideas (whether we know it or not) about what relationships are supposed to look like and much of our discomfort—feeling unloved, feeling too loved, hankering for a fight, wanting to love and being met with coolness, feeling cool when your partner wants to be loved, and so on and so on—comes in when our actual relationship diverges from these ideas.

When you were growing up you may have imagined what love would feel like or what it would mean to be in love, and by the time you were thirteen or so, you probably had a very fancy relationship movie script to go along with your ideas. This movie plays on every screen, in every theater; it is basically the only show in town. It is like you have a lens stuck in the middle of your forehead, and everywhere you look, you project your film onto the environment. Whoever walks on screen is cast in a role:

the people I see when I walk to work are extras; my mean boss is the villain; when I feel a thrill upon meeting someone new, I cast them as lover.

When you enter an actual relationship, the filmmaking goes into overdrive. At some point you may actually cease to see the real human you're in a relationship with and see only how they do or don't match your movie. When the relationship is going well, it's a sweet rom-com or meaningful drama. When it's not, it's a horror film. If you break up, you hope that Central Casting will quickly send a more suitable person to play the role of lover.

When you find yourself facing the same relationship issues over and over, it may be because you keep projecting the same scene.

If you constantly have the same arguments with different partners, you may be trapped in your script.

When you interpret everything as a good or a bad sign, need to give or get constant reassurance, continually assert your independence in the face of deepening feeling, or find yourself on the attack in the absence of anything genuinely threatening, you may be watching your movie rather than your lover.

We all know what it feels like to treat others this way—as a device rather than a person—and to be treated like this. You can tell when someone is looking right at you but not seeing you at all. We all do this to others, all day long. It is very painful and, at the same time, very ordinary.

Without meditation or a mindfulness practice of some sort, it is very difficult to manage these nuanced and ever-shifting inner states with discernment and accuracy. *With* such a practice, you can more easily detect whether you are reacting to the present moment or to your movie. When you are trapped by your narrative, mindfulness may not get you out, but at least you will know what is really going on, which enables you to be more loving toward yourself and your partner.

And ultimately, the truest love I can imagine is snapping off the projector altogether.

It takes a lot of courage to work with matters of the heart in this way. The truth is, you will be faced over and over again with choosing between your actual partner and who you imagined they could or should be. Without mindfulness, not only will you be less able to tell the difference, you run the risk of holding your partner hostage to your imaginings. When they are in sync, you will give your love. When they are not, you may withhold it. I don't know what this manner of relating to others is called, I just know it is not called love. You're going to have to choose between the vision and the person, over and over again.

Meditation, or knowing how your mind works, is the key. With mindfulness, rather than holding your partner hostage to your ideals, you let down your guard to open to them as they are. You learn to release your agenda over and over. This is love. It is much more interesting than simply getting comfortable.

To know what is happening within you, with your partner, and between you is the foundation of a relationship as a conduit of true love rather than as a contract to ensure each other's comfort. Paying attention, by the way, does not mean observing each other. It means feeling, remaining connected, close, *right there*.

When love is viewed this way, rather than wheeling and dealing love, you achieve a kind of elegance in matters of the heart. It is all predicated on your willingness to let go, return your attention to the present moment, and see what happens next.

When Paths Diverge

Some years ago, I read in the newspaper that Mattel had released a statement about Barbie. Two years earlier, apparently, Barbie had become bored with Ken and called it quits. She then hooked up with the Australian surfer Blaine. Blaine was cool! Ken was not. And what good were all her bikinis, race cars, and home furnishings without a partner to share them with, one who could really appreciate them? Ken, still with the helmet hair and snorkeling gear, was simply stuck in the past. Barbie couldn't allow herself to be held back.

Heartbroken, announced Mattel, Ken spent the Barbieless years soul-searching, "making stops in Europe and the Middle East, dabbling in Buddhism and Catholicism, teaching himself how to cook and slowly weaning himself off the beach-bum life." (I am not making this up.)

Now he had come back, refreshed and ready to reclaim Barbie, armed with a downtown wardrobe and twenty-first-century spiritual cred. I couldn't help but wonder what lay in store for this couple now that Ken had been on a search for self. Would the shoe now be on the other, less highly arched foot? Would Ken insist that Barbie also explore *her* true nature? Would he get frustrated that she refused to meditate with him, and say things like "I can't be with someone who isn't on a path"? Would Barbie feel threatened when Ken went off on retreat for a month or started hanging out with dharma dolls? Were toy meditation cushions in their future, or his-and-hers divorce attorney dolls?

On occasion, my husband and I have posed similar questions about our relationship. I am a Buddhist and he is not. Can this marriage last?

It was when our relationship was still quite new that I began to practice and study Buddhism. I set up a meditation space in my apartment, and then in our home when we began living together. Duncan was neither for nor against spiritual searching, so my pursuit was a solitary one—which I liked. (I guess I thought I could run to my shrine room and try to come back to my breath whenever things became too difficult.) Since I wasn't very involved with my Buddhist community, my refuge vows never took me too far from home. Meditation remained personal and private.

Eventually, we were married in a Buddhist ceremony, which I really wanted and he was fine with. Everything was okay. Then about five years into our marriage, I experienced unexpected and extremely gratifying professional success on a scale I never dreamed of. A book I had written with questions to ask before you get married (*The Hard Questions*) became a *New York Times* best-selling book and I was on *Oprah* and the *Today* show and whatnot. It was fabulous and exhilarating, but also scary. I realized it was time to deepen my practice. I told Duncan of my intention and went on a three-week retreat. We were both frightened that I wouldn't come home, and I almost didn't. (I considered taking monastic vows—for about ten minutes.) The following year, I went on a two-month retreat, and then another one the year after that. I made commitments to practice that were time-consuming, difficult, and joyous. Things started to heat up. I received training to become a meditation instructor. I was writing about it all. Practice and study began to inform the way I wanted to spend money, pursue friendships, and plan vacations. Gradually, I grew to long for our household to be a practice environment as well. My small shrine room had begun to feel out of place, not quite integrated with the rest of the house. My husband and stepson tiptoed and lowered their voices when they passed by. Was I becoming a stranger in my own home?

I began to seriously question our relationship. What if, say, I wanted to go off and study with a particular teacher but my husband held me back? What if the responsibilities of being in a relationship interfered with my path and he couldn't even understand why? How long before our lives simply took us in different directions? Most important, and this was the big one, how could we accompany each other as we aged and died, given that Buddhists have a particular view of old age, sickness, and death, one that I will count on to guide me, that he would be ignorant of?

During this time I ran to the shrine room a lot, trying to come back to my breath.

Here's the funny part. As I was asking these questions, Duncan didn't freak out and run away. He hung in there with me and we asked the questions together. Each time I got scared, angry, or huffy, he came back to me. Sure, he had his own fear, anger, and sense of entitlement. But somehow, unlike me, he seems to know how to recover from them, and does, quite openheartedly. So I started to as well.

Eventually I noticed that I had stopped running to my shrine room to hide. One day I looked around and realized that I was living in a practice environment and that it had happened in spite of the fact that I was making such a big deal about needing it to happen.

I've been lucky, though. I have practitioner friends in similar situations, but there's a very different vibe. I have noticed that inter-Buddhist relationships don't necessarily fare any better. In fact, there can be special difficulties. Love is very, very uncomfortable, as mentioned. It's easy to go off on retreat to avoid putting one's feet to the fire of relationship. Dharma language and practice can be used to avoid coming back to each other, whether physically or otherwise, and to cover up normal, everyday emotional puniness. I've heard friends accuse each other of being "mired in conceptuality" when really they're just irritated with each other. Or they say, "Your lovingkindness practice is weak," when what they mean is "I need some attention right now." I try to convince my husband that his reactions to my bad habits are simply a projection of his mind and that my angry words are a form of wrathful wisdom. It really does not work. He just looks at me like I'm crazy, which is actually quite helpful. And I make myself laugh when I notice how quickly my compassion for all beings disappears when I think he's driving too fast. Not that anyone has to be a saint or anything, but it's a lot easier to study love than to practice it.

I'm not saying that it doesn't make any difference whether or not your partner shares your path. It does. It really does. Understanding the powerful and precarious nature of the journey might enable you to hold and support each other in just the right way. When I meet couples who share a dharmic tribal code, it looks so wonderful and I get envious. But the parts of life that are most mysterious and uncontrollable, like falling in love, like dying, call for you to open completely in any case, without knowing how or why. Staying open requires practice. Practice requires a container, a particular place or routine without which the energy can dissipate rather quickly.

In this sense, relationships and meditation practice have a lot in common. Both begin with falling in love and then seek to stabilize a form. The forms we observe in committed relationships may vary in outward appearance, as do bowing styles and shrine ornaments, but whether we're sitting down to meditate or to fight with our spouse, following proper etiquette helps us to settle in.

In both cases, we try to recall our intentions and the instructions. We take our seat in a way that admits to both our dedication and our confusion. Most important, we acknowledge our gratitude for having fallen in love and being cracked open in any form whatsoever. The longer we practice in relationship together, the more the heat builds. Sometimes the energy is warm; other times it burns. Still, the only practice is this: gentleness, fearlessness, and the deepening of compassion for self and other. I have unshakable confidence in this truth.

Nevertheless, I pray that my faith holds, and that strange circumstances don't arise to pull me away from my meditation cushion or my husband. Of course, there are no guarantees. The more that time goes by, the more I realize how hard it is to hold any form at all (whether as dharma student or spouse), how straightforward the suggested antidotes sound, and how difficult it is to apply them. One of our Buddhist chant books contains a liturgy with these lines: "The secret gate is easily missed and so it is difficult to understand things clearly. Without the higher perceptions, one cannot realize who is at fault." What makes me cry every time I read these lines is that I know I lack the higher perceptions. I know the secret gate is right in front of me, but I can't see it, and in my blindness I increase my own and others' confusion. I'm not sure if my tears are for all sentient beings or just for Duncan, because he lives with someone who continually forgets how to love.

So whenever I start to ask myself if living with a "nonpractitioner" might be cause for concern, I try to remember how difficult it is to understand things clearly. Then I can let us both off the hook, come back, and try again to find the secret gate.

3

TRUTH #3

Meeting the Instability Together Is Love

DISCOMFORT (A.K.A. HASSLES, irritations, disconnections, misunderstandings) is your ever-present companion in a relationship. As mentioned, the Third Noble Truth states that meeting the instability together *is* love. Rather than trying to resolve it all or facing off against each other, the very best we can hope for from our partner (and it is life-changing to be able to find someone like this) is the willingness to instead turn toward the instability itself. To look at the problem as a shared entity is actually more useful than looking at it as your (or my) problem. The former reinforces your partnership while the latter creates a further division.

Real love, it seems, is a result not of feeling enraptured all the time, but of being with someone who will ride these unpredictable waves with you: Now we love each other, now we don't. Now you love me and I don't love you. Now it's the reverse. Now we feel distant from each other, now we feel close. Now we haven't a clue. And so on.

Usually, when faced with a problem, we seek to conclusively assign blame, believing that if only we could do so accurately, the problem would be solved. What if, instead of looking at each other accusingly, you shifted your gaze to the conflict itself, together? What if, instead of telling the other how they need to change so that this will never happen again, you could look at the problem as a kind of third entity that somehow landed in your house and is sitting on the couch next to you? Imagine what would happen if, instead of attacking each other, you examined the problem?

I'm not saying it is always a bad thing to address discomfort as either your issue or mine. If you are always late (and that pisses me off), you could work on trying to be on time rather than getting me to stop being mad about it. If you are irritated by my absent-mindedness, I could try to be more organized. These are common courtesies that thoughtful people extend to each other and, in intimate relationships, good manners have unending value. But other kinds of discomfort are about ways your behavior interferes with my fantasy of what a relationship should look like. In such cases, instead of continually trying to make the other person into who we want them to be or feeling that we should turn into the person that they need—which is a fool's errand—what seems to be more useful is to open to the crazy, unpredictable flow of energy between the two of you and identify problems as you would a sudden leak in a boat. Knowing nothing whatsoever about seafaring, I still guess that sailors fix a leak first and attempt to identify the cause second, not as a gesture of contempt but as one of preparedness. In so doing, skill, awareness, and knowledge increase. In boating this may be navigational expertise, but in a relationship it is called intimacy.

Of course, some issues are true deal breakers. If you want to have children and your partner does not, there is no compromise, no middle ground. Or if you have religious beliefs that the other person doesn't share, you may still love him or her but that is not the kind of life you want to have. Some sources of instability are not workable, and each couple must make such determinations on their own. Outside of such situations, looking together at discomfort is more than a good relationship strategy. It is a cornerstone of love.

The Container Principle

This is not easy. In fact, though we seek relationships in order to find ease and satisfaction, it is actually the most difficult area of life in which to find such things. We become extremely confused about what is supposed to happen in a relationship. Though we may be geniuses at solving problems at work or with our friends, when problems arise in love, our elevated viewpoints evaporate and we resort to fancy adult hissy fits. No one, it seems, is immune: not therapists, ministers, beauty queens, captains of industry, or our post-therapy selves. Forget about Smith & Wesson—relationships are the great equalizer. That said, we can work with it all by keeping in mind the "container principle."

The container principle is the idea that the environment you establish or find yourself in can influence or even give rise to an outcome—and that what happens in a particular space changes the "feel" of that space. For example, when you practice meditation in a church or temple, it feels different than when you practice alone at home or on the bus. You are still you and the practice is still the practice; the best explanation for the qualitative difference in your experience is the space itself. If you practice consistently in the same spot, eventually that spot begins to feel powerful. You can feel your meditation begin as you walk up to it. When you eat your dinner standing over the sink, it may actually taste different than when you are seated at a table with linens and lovely music. If you want to have a difficult conversation with someone, it feels one way to do it in person and another when done via email. These are all examples of containers.

The space in which your relationship takes place can have palpable influence on the relationship itself. Say you're on a date with someone who is beautiful, smart, and funny, and the conversation has been delightful. They invite you to their home and you agree to go. What would you then feel about them if you walked into a luxurious, clean, and beautiful apartment? a McMansion? a basement bedroom in their parents' home? In all cases, the conversation would change. Whether that would be for better or worse depends on your associations.

When it comes to relationships, something interesting happens when we expand our view of solving problems to include not just your behavior and my behavior and a deep understanding of our family-of-origin issues, but also the environment in which our relationship is taking place. Space is constructed of physical and nonphysical materials. The former are up to you. When it comes to the latter, the energetic structure you create to house your love can be built bit by bit, courtesy by courtesy, kiss by kiss. What follows are suggestions for creating the space where love wants to live.

Five Steps to Develop a Strong Container

We spend a fair amount of our days doing so-called ordinary things: keeping house (or avoiding it), getting dressed, eating meals, hanging out. It's normal to think of our spiritual or romantic life as separate from all of this, but it is not. By taking five very ordinary, simple steps, you can actually make everyday life a container for your spiritual life. When you do, the way you live on a day-to-day basis, rather than being draining or confusing, can become a source of power.

My teacher, Sakyong Mipham, taught me the following five steps for developing such a container. Anyone can do these five things. They may sound very simple, but they are not. Though they are about how you conduct yourself individually in the most ordinary circumstances, I have also found them to be really useful when it comes to relationships. Let's look at each step on its own, then apply them to relationships.

Clean up your space. When you live in chaos, you feel chaotic. It's hard to feel energized and together when you are stepping over undifferentiated piles of stuff. When you make your space orderly (according to your definition of "orderly"), the impact on vitality is dramatic.

Wear nice clothes. I thought this meant I had to go out and buy a whole new wardrobe. For better or worse, it does not. It simply means to wear clothes that are clean and pressed, fit you well, and make you feel cheerful. In other words, don't pick up yesterday's clothes off the floor, put them on, and think, "This is good enough." Take some care in the way you dress yourself, not necessarily to appear fashionable or make a statement, but as an expression of self-regard.

Eat good food. This does not mean becoming a vegan or doing a detox fast. It means that when you buy, prepare, and consume food (and drink), make sure it is of the best quality you can afford or find, procured decently, prepared thoughtfully, and consumed with appreciation. Take care and pay attention to what and how you eat. If you *want* to be vegan, buy fresh vegetables and organic grains. If you want to eat a burger, rather than shoveling in a McAnything, get quality meat. If you want to drink coffee, get good beans, and if you want to drink tequila, buy a nice bottle. To nourish yourself with quality is a sign of respect and changes the quality of your presence.

Spend time with people who like or love you and whom you like or love. Requires no explanation, right? Still, we all have to spend time with people we'd rather not, and this suggestion is not a directive to cut those people out of your life. Rather, minimize the amount of time you spend with such individuals or groups and maximize the time you spend with those for whom, when you are with them, you see yourself (and them) as wonderful, interesting, or lovable.

If you ignore all the other steps and just do this one, I believe you will be amazed at the difference it makes in the way you view yourself and how much energy you have.

Spend time in the natural world. Our world is good. Cold is cold. Purple is purple. Water is wet. When we touch in with what is most elemental, we remember the simplicity and depth of our experience here on Planet Earth.

Each of these five steps reminds us to slow down and pay attention to ourselves, others, and the world with love in our hearts. When applied to relationships, their power expands exponentially.

1. CLEAN UP YOUR SHARED SPACE.

The home is the body of your relationship—it is what you can both see, relate to, take care of, or destroy. It is the relationship made tangible.

Once I went with Duncan to visit some friends who lived in a super-wealthy suburb of Boston. As we drove down their street, I saw mansion after mansion—not the McMansion sort, but the old-school New England, Gothic

Revival, 1800s sort. Sloping manicured lawns, stables, old fir trees... you get the picture. He mentioned to me that his friends had become avid art collectors, which sounded interesting. Indeed, when we walked in we were greeted by paintings, sculptures, ceramics, tapestries, and so on. The marble and wood entryway featured beautiful molding everywhere. However, there were also piles of unsorted laundry in various corners, a bunch of strange-looking stuff in the kitchen sink, and an accompanying odor whose provenance I tried not to guess. The exterior said "We're rich," but the feeling inside was "Who gives a sh*t?"

On a different occasion we were going to visit an old family friend of Duncan's parents who had lived in Manhattan's East Village since the 1960s. I don't know what her reasons were, but at some point Marian Miller became a Zen practitioner named Marian Miller Minuski who lived in one of the last rent-controlled apartments in Manhattan. Duncan had not seen her in decades so we were not sure what to expect. We arrived at her apartment, a nondescript five-story walk-up that seemed to be all fire escapes. We climbed the stairs to the top floor and knocked on her door. She was quite old by this time, gray hair in a wispy bun, a cardigan with a tissue tucked in the cuff, the whole nine yards. Her apartment was very spare. The sofa today might be called "midcentury modern," but really it was just an old couch. The rugs were threadbare. There were roughhewn wood shelves for books and knick-knacks. Marian invited us to sit on the couch while she went into the kitchen to get tea and cookies. Lipton and Chips Ahoy, I believe.

To this day, I cannot explain what I then experienced. The tea tasted rich and peaty. *Hey, I've had Lipton before,*

I thought, *but it never tasted like this. And these cookies—what is in them? They are fantastic!* The gimcracks on her shelves seemed to glow, and if I had picked one up, I would have wanted to handle it with great care. As we conversed, I found myself sitting up straighter. Our conversation—about nothing more than the weather, old friends, NYC rents—seemed to slow and deepen and I paid close attention to everything she said. I looked around and realized that I was in a palace and she was a queen. The outside said "low-income," but the feeling inside was of royalty.

Forgive the terribly clichéd example of superficial rich people who actually have nothing versus humble old people who possess what really matters—but how did Marian Miller Minuski create such an environment of richness?

The answer is elegance. True elegance expresses itself organically through the act of *caring*. Though we live in a society that prizes effortlessness, disposability, and a "don't care" mentality, there is far more to be had by looking after what is yours—your body, your home, your stuff, your guests—as if it all mattered. Ms. Minuski had spent decades caring for and caring about what was hers, and at some point the environment became an expression of her heart. It was palpable and unforgettable.

This is the power that environment has to create our reality: it can actually change the way food tastes, light shines, and people listen.

Have you ever wondered why so many (so many!) arguments start because someone leaves a pile of dirty dishes in the sink, will not clean the lint out of the drier, or continues to collect and display Star Wars action figures all over the house? These are very small issues in the great scheme of things. (Well, maybe not the Star Wars action figures.) Yet they have the power to hurt, to enrage, and to destroy the vibe. Whenever two people occupy one space with different senses of propriety and beauty (which is basically always), a negotiation must take place. That negotiation is most often unstated; instead it is expressed in evil looks, aggressive acquisitions, or simple withdrawal to a preferred corner. The negotiation can be brutish, as when one person simply ignores the other's wishes and the former ends up feeling like they are living in someone else's home. Or it can be absurdly picayune—every single item in every single corner is subjected to lengthy debate until agreement is reached or someone just gives up in exhaustion. The point I'm making is that the way we inhabit space together is rarely about knick-knacks or color schemes. It is about caring and thoughtfulness.

As mentioned previously, during the first years of our marriage, we lived in two different cities: New York City (me) and Boston (him). During this time, we bought a house together in a dreaded (by me) location called Arlington, Massachusetts. Nothing wrong with Arlington. It's a sweet little town very close to both Boston and Cambridge—but I hated it. I do not care for a suburban-like atmosphere and this was 101 percent suburbia. Anyway, I will not go into detail about all the things I did not love about Arlington. What was important at this time in life was to live somewhere with a good public school system so that my stepson could get a decent education. It was most definitely the right thing to do. But I would never feel at home there. (We lived there for ten years.)

So I was already not starting on the good foot. In addition, my husband was the primary resident of this home, as I only spent half my time there. Over the first few years, all the little decisions that go into creating a household—how to organize the dishes in the kitchen, what was stored in the basement, whether to paint the front steps light or dark gray—were made by him. This was totally understandable. But the net result was that I felt I was living in someone else's home. These little details of creating a household are actually more important than deciding what goes where. They create a kind of intimacy with the space and this is what makes it feel like home. The combination of not loving the setting and not being privy to the day-to-day micro-decisions made about this or that created a great sense of unease for me, and, therefore, for him. When, after my stepson graduated high school, we finally moved, I was intent on creating our new household in a different way, which we did. Whether it was because we had moved to the city or gotten older or came to know each other better, because my Mercury crossed over his Mars, or whatever, in our new home we definitely argued less and loved each other more.

2. DRESS WITH CARE (EVEN AFTER YOU'VE BEEN TOGETHER FOREVER).

I happen to be married to someone who loves clothes—partly, I suppose, because he is tall and wiry and everything looks good on him. Or because he is a Leo. Or he just likes clothing, who knows. It has nothing to do with fashion. Rather, I would say it has to do with decorum. He has an inherent sense of dignity about his person.

It is one thing to dress to impress, attract, or insult (yes, that's possible—clothing is that powerful), but it is another to dress the way you do because you appreciate yourself and your clothing. To do so expresses a very particular quality that at one time was highly prized but is now largely forgotten and unremarked upon: a quality called dignity. Your parents or grandparents may have suggested things like "Sit up straight," "Don't mumble," or "Put on some clean clothes, for goodness' sake." On one hand, they were trying to help you to become civilized, but on the other, such edicts are also instructions in dignity. When you are in possession of it, you naturally sit up straight, speak clearly, and wear clean clothes. No one has to tell you to do this. And when you feel sad, angry, frustrated, you may take it out on your dignity by slouching around, muttering, clad in yesterday's tracksuit. We've all been there. When you spend time with another person, such things are strangely contagious. They have the power to create an ambience that is uplifted and inviting or kind of seamy and uncertain. The way you clothe yourself (and the care you take of your clothing) makes a difference.

3. SHARE FOOD TOGETHER WITH DELIGHT.

What is more fundamental to a relationship than sharing a meal? As life becomes busier and busier, the sweetness of sharing food together is easy to lose. It becomes habitual (we always eat dinner at seven/together/apart), prescriptive (to improve health or build muscle), or boring. ("How was your day?" "Fine." "How was yours?" "Fine." *Silence.*) It seems that the joy has gone out of eating. We're scared of food for various reasons, whether because we think it may cause weight gain or illness, because it's not "clean" enough, or because sugar is the devil. Rather than eating for pleasure, we eat for control or reward, and dining has become transactional. We may have lost sight of what it could be: a way of spending time together without any particular agenda. (For more on recovering a sense of elegance in your relationship to food and nourishment, please see the work of my great friend Jenna Hollenstein, founder of Eat to Love.) Rather than being a meeting to discuss bills, household issues, and schedules, sharing food could be a time to let go of all of that and simply converse. How are you? What have you been thinking about? What's been going on with you that is funny or sad? What are you looking forward to or dreading? Any open-ended questions that give two people a chance to simply be together.

Sakyong Mipham, my teacher, is a traditionally educated Tibetan who came to the West as a teenager, so he is truly a blend of both cultures. Around ten years ago, he married a traditionally educated Tibetan woman. She suggested they have tea together every day in the late afternoon. *What for?* he wondered. After a time, he realized that it was for the purpose of—wait for it—conversation. Not to bargain. Not to discuss. Not to present or pontificate, measure or dutifully check in. Simply to talk. He came to see that being together in this uncomplicated way, just chatting, eating and drinking, sitting across from each other, was actually adding to the weave of love, home, and commitment. Each thread—of ordinary words exchanged, sips of black tea, food appreciated, opening up to each other—reinforced the tapestry. The relationship deepened, not by interpersonal breakthroughs or working through issues, but by being together in this elemental way. PS: If you'd like to read more about Sakyong Mipham's journey into the world of relationships (which is truly edifying), please read his book *The Lost Art of Good Conversation.*

4. SPEND TIME ENJOYING EACH OTHER'S GOOD QUALITIES.

Notice what you love or admire about this person and spend a little time expanding your appreciation of those qualities. In Buddhist thought, this way of noticing is called "contemplation." To contemplate someone's lovely qualities does not mean to think about them. It has more to do with focusing on the quality you wish to contemplate and resting with it as it echoes and moves about in your mind. Feel into it rather than analyze it. Just like with the breath in formal sitting practice, when you notice you have strayed into thought (*I wish he was always like this, I should become more like her*, and so on), let go and resume attention on the felt sense of this lovely quality.

Since we have probably already spent a lot of time in contemplation of that person's impatience, dullness, anger, bad habits, and so on, we have the mechanism in place for contemplation of their beauty. The machine is strong. It is simply a matter of switching out the inputs. (To make this switch, by the way, a steady meditation practice is irreplaceable. Just saying.)

5. SPEND TIME TOGETHER IN THE NATURAL WORLD.

I am an inveterate city person. To me, going outside means walking to the coffee shop. When I was a child, my favorite thing to do was lie on the couch and read. Invariably, my mother would say, "It's a beautiful day—why don't you go outside and enjoy it?" I would think, *I am enjoying it.*

From right here. As an adult, I have not changed much, so when Duncan first suggested cross-country skiing after a big snowfall here in New England, my initial reaction was, *Why on earth would we do that?!* Bless his heart, he talked me into it: I went grudgingly, and only after promises of treats, snacks, and rewards. (I can be very lazy.) Needless to say (otherwise I would not be telling this story), we had a fantastic time skiing across fields and through woods. If before this little jaunt my mind had been grumbling with checklists, chores, and all the things I did not like about myself and my life, afterward I was in incredibly good cheer. When, together, you can take your attention off the minutiae of everyday life to remember that in addition to emails and groceries, the world also has trees, lakes, forests, sun, and mountains, perspective automatically resets itself and your true priorities are more easily recalled.

The Four Immeasurables

The Four Immeasurables, or *Brahmaviharas* (royal dwelling places), refer to the inner states where it is most valuable to reside. Normally, we may reside in places that are far less exalted: in anger, crankiness, insecurity, and so on. To rest in inner darkness creates an inner home of darkness. To rest in inner goodness creates an inner home of goodness. It is pretty simple.

There are four such places within all of us. (Yes, all of us.) They have no limit and are thus called immeasurable.

The first brahmavihara is *lovingkindness*, which means to recognize that all beings—*all*: human, animal, insect, fish, seen, unseen, past, present, future—are alike in that they simply want to be happy, healthy, safe, and peaceful. Some go about it in very sensible ways, while others seek it in ways that are completely insane and worse. Nonetheless, our core motivation is the same. This is very good news. With lovingkindness we recognize our commonality. Genuine warmth arises naturally. With this warmth, we are able to avoid consigning some beings to the category called "us" and others to the cemetery known as "them." Lovingkindness is completely essential because with "us" there is hope of connection and with "them" all manner of violence is possible.

Though we may think that a relationship is about love above all else, true lovingkindness can be forgotten in the midst of everyday trials and tribulations. To remember that your beloved is simply trying to find happiness just as you are is actually an ancient teaching on what it means to love. You will find such a teaching in every one of the world's wisdom traditions. Every version of the Golden Rule is about this: thinking of others as you would yourself and recognizing your commonality.

The second brahmavihara is *compassion*, which means to feel someone else's pain in your own heart. This is not the same thing as feeling sorry for anyone or, upon hearing, say, that someone has lost their job, imagining what you would feel in such a circumstance and then mapping that complex of feelings over to them to arrive at the conclusion "Oh, that is awful." Nothing wrong with that, but compassion is actually more immediate. It is literally as if that person's pain has become part of who you are in that moment. You feel it viscerally, wordlessly. It is a shared space, not a hot potato.

When you love someone, you know exactly what is meant here. Their sorrows touch you in ways that can feel unbearable. The more you can relax with this, the more you can love. To welcome another's pain into your own heart is at the pinnacle of what it means to love.

The third immeasurable quality, *sympathetic joy*, works in the same exact way as compassion, but rather than feeling another's pain as your own, you feel their happiness as your own. Suddenly you see that you have access to an incalculable source of riches. You don't have to rely on your own machinations to provide satisfying moments from time to time; all of the joy in the world actually belongs to you already because you can feel it in your own heart, no matter what.

The fourth royal dwelling place is *equanimity*, which speaks to a kind of steadiness of heart that permits you to ride these incessant waves of love, sorrow, and joy without ever shutting down. Yes, it may seem unimaginable, but according to Buddhist thought any other possibilities are unimaginable. The Four Immeasurables are a complete road map to the realm of love.

Six Transcendent Actions

If the Four Immeasurables point to indestructible qualities of the heart, the Six Paramitas (or transcendent actions) tell us how to express these qualities in practical terms. They provide a guide for creating a lasting relationship by continually reinforcing the container.

Generosity

Earlier, we discussed the power of releasing your agenda over and over as a prerequisite for loving. In so doing, you open to your actual partner rather than to your ideas of who you wished they were. Sometimes this is wonderful. Sometimes it is not. Still, you have declared your allegiance to love rather than illusion, and this is extremely powerful. Perennial return to a state of openness, while potentially terrifying, is also the gateway to generosity. Generosity with an agenda ("You owe me"; "Being nice to you enables me to think well of myself"; "Now you can't leave me"...) is a gambit to gain an advantageous position. Generosity without agenda is, well, generosity.

Absent an agenda, it is possible to view and offer generosity as what it really is: a gesture of confidence, love, and largesse. Generosity is regal. It is nontransactional, liberated from scorekeeping, and free of manipulation because it is based in unconditioned openness.

In the West we may hear the suggestion to be generous as an admonition to never think of yourself. For some reason, we've gotten the idea that generosity is a "me or you" situation and that if the thought of gaining anything in return even enters our mind, the benevolence is fully negated. (Buddhist teachings concur on this point. However, not only do they posit that true giving is devoid of a giver, they also posit that it is devoid of a recipient and a gift. Go figure.) When generosity is offered according to any conceptual view, then, it may look like a caress but feel like a punch in the face. To avoid this, take the focus off of giver, recipient, and score and look instead at the creation of the gift. When you focus on what you can offer rather than on what the offering means, you become one with the generous impulse.

Only good can come of this.

In Buddhist thought, truly generous gifts take one of three forms:

THE GIFT OF MATERIAL GOODS

This is what we commonly think of as generosity, and it is indeed important and powerful, even life-changing. If someone is hungry, you give them food; if they are poor, you give them money; and if they are cold, you give them a coat. It is very simple.

The gift of material goods is central in any relationship because it touches us at a primal level. We all need food, shelter, and warmth to survive. To commit to a relationship is to take on the responsibility and honor of preserving each other's lives. That is a very straightforward part of the bargain. While it used to be the primary chip, its power has become diluted as the relationship game has expanded from "Let's pool our resources so we don't get eaten by panthers" to "Let's pool our resources so we can buy a home." In any case, to whatever degree each couple decides, the pool of resources is now shared. Resources (or their absence) can create or, quite literally, destroy lives.

The power of this form of generosity is invoked each time you pay household bills, or wash each other's clothes, sleep under the same covers, and so on. To imbue such actions with the energy of life-affirming generosity rather than see them as boring chores that make you cranky can turn the most ordinary household activities into tiny gestures of kindness. Such gestures accrue. If you want to walk into your home and feel that it is a true sanctuary, a fueling station for basic sanity, and a place that love wants to live, pay closer attention to the way you make your bed, do your laundry, spend your money, and eat your meals—not to prove a point, fulfill a contract, or make everything pretty, but out of respect for the sacred charge of protecting each other's well-being and as the gesture of a loving heart.

THE GIFT OF FEARLESSNESS

In the Buddhist view, fearlessness is not about thinking you can handle everything. It has nothing to do with believing in yourself or trusting the universe, although both of those things are fantastic. Rather, fearlessness arises organically when you remember that you are at heart an ethical, loving, capable, unique, brilliant, caring, joyous, powerful, and generous human being. Why do I say so? Because you were born that way. All evidence to the contrary is the result of being hurt by those who have forgotten their own true nature and so act in ways that are stupid, harmful, and worse.

Love seems custom-made to evoke the deepest woundings and thereby forces you to choose over and over between your puny/fearful self and your heroic/genius self. The closer you get to another person, the louder your sorrows shriek, the more frightened you become, the more you scare each other, all resulting in some very weird battles that have nothing to do with what is actually happening.

For example, someone I know—let's call him Shmuncan—has a particular sensitivity to not being listened to because he grew up in a household of five kids with two working parents where attention was always stretched and dinnertime conversation revolved around winning arguments, which was considered a spectacular feat. I mean, no one likes to go unheard, especially in argumentative situations, but the slightest evidence of such can invoke in Shmuncan a significant fury. When he speaks to his partner—let's call her Shmusan—he checks her response for specific proof that what he has said has been understood exactly as he meant it, and I mean *to the letter*. Shmusan has a history of being considered, shall we say, lacking in certain intellectual capacities due to her difficulty (later diagnosed as a learning disorder) in choosing from among all the possible interpretations of a particular statement, making traditional education a torture chamber. Though she comes from a family of five with eight higher degrees among them, she did not go to college because it would have been a fiasco. So she has spent a lot of time feeling stupid for not being able to understand what others had no trouble with, and is therefore perfectly matched with Shmuncan, who has a near-pathological fear of being misunderstood. They have argued, despaired, felt extremely unloved by each other, and, I would say, even hated each other—all rooted in fears that have lived on far beyond their expiration dates.

To give the gift of fearlessness in a relationship is not to baby each other and try to make up for what was lost by oversupplying it, tiptoeing around it, or creating endless allowances for it to play itself out. You can't snuggle your way out of such a situation, nor is analyzing each other particularly helpful when the intention is to diagnose rather than to love. (I often think of my friend Greg's assessment of his family's three-step problem-solving methodology: 1. Define problem. 2. Assign blame. 3. Problem solved.)

Generosity here is to recognize what each is provoking in the other and then separate what is connected to present circumstances (it's true, sometimes Shmusan does not listen to Shmuncan) and what stems from days of yore. In this way, you demonstrate that what you encounter is workable and every relationship disconnect does not necessarily spell the end of love. Your courage in turning toward what is difficult to face naturally imparts such courage to others.

THE GIFT OF DHARMA

When Duncan and I first talked about getting married, I had a lot of questions. (So many, it turned out, that they became a book, *The Hard Questions: 100 Essential Questions to Ask before You Say "I Do."* Poor Duncan!) My questions weren't about whether or not we loved each other. They were about how we would create a life together. Where would we live? Would we celebrate holidays? Keep our money in the same bank account?

While we had healthy agreement on some questions and tolerable disagreement on others, our response to this last question was: Me, without hesitation: *No.* Him, equally unhesitatingly: *Yes.* What? Why would we put our money together? I had my own business. He had been through a complicated divorce. It would be so much simpler to just keep our money separate. Plus, I didn't really want anyone poking through my finances/hair salon bills. I was surprised that he was shocked and hurt by my answer. He wondered how we would then pay our bills and divide up expenses. I said something about how we would figure it out. Then he asked me, "Are you going to have your own milk carton in the refrigerator?" and this was the question that stopped my mind. With that, I saw that the path I was inviting us down was one of separation. What he proposed was a path of merging.

This is a very small example of what is meant by giving the gift of dharma, which is not about explaining a philosophy or sharing knowledge—it is about opening someone's mind to a different way, one based in a bigger view.

Discipline

When many people hear the word "discipline" in the context of a relationship, they think that what is meant is a strict adherence to a system of thought that, if observed diligently, will prevent or resolve emotional conflicts.

Some systems contain wonderful counsel, such as advocating that couples always seek to compromise, make sure to spend enough time together (or apart), or observe the same rituals or religion. But while these suggestions can be useful, they don't seem to have anything to do with love. When taken with an agenda, even the agenda to create a better relationship, such actions fail to connect with love's transcendent properties.

I am proposing an alternative view of discipline. Discipline in a relationship is working with each individual situation that arises with integrity and openness. It means taking the largest view possible of the relationship itself, again and again. This view is rooted in trust in each other's basic sanity and the certainty that, over and above our inadequacies, we each possess a kind of brilliance.

When you and your beloved have the discipline to trust in each other's goodness and basic sanity first and the truth of your flaws second, there is the possibility that the difficulties you experience will self-liberate, meaning that they will find resolution organically or simply cease to be relevant. So when you find yourself becoming mired in a theory about why a difficulty has arisen, try this: Don't abandon the theory. Look at it. Examine your views. Take them seriously. Then let them go. The discipline here is to come back to your beloved with open eyes and to see them as they are right now, without having an agenda to change them or yourself.

Patience

Patience doesn't just mean tolerance for your beloved's frailties, nor does it mean maintaining hope in the face of repeating arguments over the exact same issues. It has more to do with tolerance for your own frailties first, a willingness to take on and work with your own mind.

You could say that all relationship difficulties begin with the unwillingness to face our own emotions. It is painful to me when I feel inadequate, unappreciated, invisible—and this pain is real. However, it is a mistake (that is, not helpful) to assign responsibility for my feelings to my husband, no matter how much of a jerk I may perceive him to be in any given moment. Patience has more to do with becoming solely and always responsible for my own emotional reactions.

The sitting practice of meditation is the most direct method I know for adopting such a relationship into your own inner life. I'm pretty sure that without it I wouldn't have been able to make space for the extraordinary holograms of emotion that come and go during even a single day as partners.

Exertion

When I was getting married, I read a lot of books and articles about how to have a successful relationship. I mean, look around. Not many people get it right.

Almost all of the advice I got from books, friends, and family boiled down to a single dictum: *Relationships take work*. I have to say, this did not make me happy. Not that I have anything against work, but when I looked at my sweet boyfriend and imagined that all our effortless love and passion, the easy delight we took in each other, was somehow, through marriage, going to become a kind of drudgery, I thought, *Wait, what? How does that happen? And how can I avoid it at all costs?*

The Buddhist view of exertion provides a few clues. Rather than implying drudgery, exertion is synonymous with joy. It's not about working hard to make problems go away or trying your very best at all times. It is so much simpler than that. Here, exertion is the noble act of taking an interest. When you get along, you take an interest in that. When you don't, you take an interest in that, too. You take an interest when you are able to connect with your beloved openly, gracefully, and easily, and also when you connect to them with grumpiness, selfishness, and a sense of entitlement. Taking an interest is not about reductive analysis or figuring out what is going on so you can be done with it. It is a way of opening to your own experience—and to your beloved—with tenderness and honesty. It is the act of continuously disposing of your ideas about love to instead live your experience of love fully, which gives rise to vitality, energy, and joy.

Exertion, as Chögyam Trungpa defined it, is to "work unceasingly with our own neurosis and speed." Who doesn't want to be married to someone who does that? When I know that my husband is committed to work in this way, whether he succeeds or fails in any particular instance, I not only trust him, my heart melts toward him.

Meditation

In meditation practice, the breath is the object of attention. You train yourself to notice when the mind strays from the breath, let go of what it has strayed to, and then return to the breath. Our practice in a relationship is similar, but instead of the breath, love itself is our mutual object of attention. When attention strays into rage, disconnection, resentment—or even affection, delight, and passion—we come back to love. By "love," I don't mean any particular feeling. Perhaps "opening" is a better word. When my husband pisses me off with his unbelievably hypercritical comments, or I irritate the crap out of him with my self-absorption or complete lack of spatial awareness, I'm not suggesting that he or I drop our feelings and try to be sweet and nice to each other. I'm suggesting that we simply open to each other. Again. Again. Again.

Who is he to me right now? Someone I love. And now? Someone I despise. Someone who bores me. Inspires me. Soothes me. And who is he right now, and right now, as best I can tell? Someone who feels happy. Sad. Alone. Confused. When it comes to love, the best you can hope for (and it is far better than whatever you may imagine, based on movies and whatnot) is not someone for whom you feel love all the time—or passion or admiration—but someone who will take your hand and step with you into the insane flood of need and desire and emotion and connection and, with eyes wide open, watch it all and feel it fully. Together.

To become each other's object of meditation is a good problem-solving methodology when it comes to relationships. As with formal meditation practice, the right combination of closeness and relaxation is essential. This is not easy. It takes near-superhuman strength and energy. It will become exhausting, there is no doubt. You will encounter the same problems over and over. You will think something has been resolved but find that it hasn't been. You will be constantly heartened and disheartened, delighted and disappointed. That seems to be the game. When people say "Relationships take work!" this is the kind of work they mean. If you're willing to do it, you are in fantastic shape. If you're not—and I totally understand and appreciate anyone who would answer in the negative—marriage might not be for you. Contrary to every song, book, movie, and advertisement ever created, it is not for everyone. It really does take work. Whether that is good or bad depends on your perspective.

Wisdom

In all my thinking about the nature of wisdom over two decades of Buddhist study, there is only one thing I can say about it with any confidence: It has nothing to do with me or my little understandings or insights (not that there is anything wrong with them). It has more to do, it seems, with giving up on the idea of "my" wisdom and instead making a relationship to wisdom itself, the field of intelligence that underlies, encapsulates, gives rise to, is utterly indifferent to and also madly in love with "me."

When I try to love my husband from a place of thinking that I know what is going on between us or understand what love is, I fail to connect with him. When I am able to disengage from my ideas about who either of us is or should be or what love itself should look like and instead meet him in a place beyond knowing, I see again and again that wisdom, groundlessness, and love are absolutely inseparable. So—whether our connection feels joyous, contentious, dull, or shocking—we begin again. And again.

After all the fights, daily irritations, and completely unpredictable disappearances and resurgences of love and desire, I have given up trying to analyze or control what makes us argue or reconcile. Instead, the best I can do is look at each disconnect, the teeny ones and the seemingly insurmountable ones, as yet another chance to step beyond my comfort zone and into a deeper love. When I try to hold our relationship in the cradle of lovingkindness in just this way, our difficulties become ornaments in the crazy dance of love.

The Placement of Attention

Poet and Zen priest John Tarrant, Roshi, once said, "Attention is the most basic form of love. Through it we bless and are blessed." I cannot tell you how true I find these words to be. To shine the light of your awareness on your beloved is not only the foundation of love, it *is* love. Without the willingness or ability to do so, love is simply not possible. In this sense, the ability to understand, modulate, and discern where your attention is and how, should you wish, to shift it may be the most important factor in being truly loving.

As a Buddhist and a meditator, I have trained for many years in placement of attention, also known as mindfulness meditation. In fact, that is all that is meant by mindfulness: agile placement of attention. This word, mindfulness, has taken on enormous significance in the last decade as a solution to countless problems, from getting a better night's sleep to becoming a better leader or improving your golf game. But all mindfulness really means is the ability to place your attention on an object of your choosing and then (and this is the kicker) to hold it there. This is becoming an increasingly rarified skill, I am sure I don't have to tell you. When it comes to love, as mentioned above, this skill is essential. If you can't pay attention, quite literally, you cannot love.

Although it may sound obvious, it often goes unnoticed that people pay attention to different things in the same situation. For example, if we were to walk into a restaurant together, I might notice the noise level first while you immediately scan for an empty table. If we go for a drive, you may focus on enjoying the scenery while I am engaged in reaching the destination. If we fall in love, you might be most concerned with shared values while I just want to have fun. None of these objects of attention are better than the others, but to assume that what I focus on is what you naturally focus on (or should) is to open the door to a world of confusion. If there is one thing I could teach everyone on earth about how to be in a relationship, it is this: to learn to see clearly what engages another's attention and to discern accurately where you meet and where you diverge. I have become convinced that this is the key to love, peace, and well-being in all relationships. I am not even exaggerating!

What I am about to share with you here is drawn from my longtime study of the Enneagram, a system of typology. Though the Enneagram has nothing to do with traditional Buddhist teachings, for me they are deeply connected.

The Buddhist view is that anything that creates more love, wisdom, and confidence is an *upaya*, or "skillful means." Skillful means could look like anything: a warm embrace, a slap in the face, offering advice, remaining silent, and so on. Skillful means are pointed, precise, effective, and in the moment. They are not planned as much as they are simply offered on the spot, based on mindfulness and awareness. The Four Immeasurables are an *upaya*, as are the Six Paramitas.

In relationships with my partner, friends, family, and students, there has been no greater *upaya* than the Enneagram. I use it every day of my life. It enables me to connect with people I love and people I dislike. It helps me to see the difference between my way of doing things and everyone else's, not to one-up anyone (goodness knows my way is riddled with kinks) but to pierce the veil of self-absorption and see beyond it. Though a thorough exploration of the Enneagram is well beyond the scope of this book, I would be remiss if I didn't share with you what, to me, is an essential piece of the puzzle.

The Enneagram posits the following:

There are nine styles of attention.

There are three primary instinctual drives that we all share, but one is primary for most of us.

There are three possible responses to threats that we all utilize, but one is primary for most of us.

I'm going to share a bit about each of these in exceptionally broad strokes. (You do not have to study the Enneagram or have any interest whatsoever in systems of typology to benefit from this intelligence, but if you are intrigued by this material, there are reading suggestions in Appendix B. And if you find such things to be dull and silly, skip ahead!)

Very loosely, these are the nine categories of things a person might attend to in any given situation, whether going to a party, choosing a career, deciding who to vote for, or how to win a fight. Clearly, they are very broad. As you read through them, see if you can find the style of attention that sounds most like your own.

1. RIGHT OR WRONG

When this is your attention style, focus automatically goes to what is being done, said, or experienced correctly or incorrectly. This person has what in Buddhist thought is called "comparing mind," meaning he or she possesses an internal sense of right and wrong and is constantly weighing what he or she does, says, or experiences against it. When there is congruence, they can relax. When there is not, a disturbance in the field is created. This is the sort of person who, when they like you, tells you what you are doing wrong. Because who would not love that?!

The other day, I received an email from a member of my online community, the Open Heart Project, that began with how much she had benefited from my meditation instruction. It was so heartfelt. How lovely! She went on to say that if I wanted make it even better, I could make a few improvements and she went on to enumerate what she found to be subpar in my life's work. When you receive such a message from a stranger, it could piss you off. And it did! A little. But I could also feel that her intention was somehow meant to express gratitude, which, for her, was telling me what bothered her about my work so I could fix it. Yes, for some people, this is seen as a gift. Whether it was or was not, I chose to respond to it in that way and thanked her.

This, by the way, is Duncan's primary style of attention. (It is also my mother's, so I know this style quite well.) To know this about him has been extremely useful in our relationship, especially when it comes to the fights we have. When we are about to have an argument, I try to identify something I have done that he considers "wrong" and immediately confess to it. I don't lie or take responsibility for something I have not done, but when I am able to acknowledge the right and wrong in whatever is upsetting him, he lowers his guard and we can have a real conversation. If I am unable to do that, he will keep pressing the same point over and over.

When this kind of person speaks to you about something difficult, it may sound like a lecture because they want you to understand the underlying morality of their perspective. When you speak to them, it is useful to indicate some awareness of this moral component.

The difficult news about this style of attention is that it is very black and white.

The great news is that you can trust this person because they are vehemently opposed to wrongdoing. They will stand up for what they believe and will not back down. What does our world need right now more than people whose integrity is beyond dispute? This style models that for the rest of us.

2. WHAT IS NEEDED?

This is a very different style of attention from the one above. Rather than scanning for what is correct or incorrect, this person scans for what they can offer any given situation or person. They have an uncanny ability to sense what is needed. When this person has your best interests at heart, this is unbelievably lovely. When they don't, it is unbelievably manipulative.

In reading this book, for example, rather than searching for what will help them to love more deeply, a person with this attention style may first look for what will be useful to those they know so that they may share it. Again, lovely. But when "offering what is needed" is a person's primary communication tool, it is used for everything: to express love, certainly, but also to express disdain, distance, anger, and so on. It can be tricky to discern it when you are with this kind of person, but a good clue is when you constantly find yourself on the receiving end (of gifts, favors, ideas, and so on) but it is decidedly one way—any attempt to offer something in return is somehow shut down.

When this person wants to discuss something painful, they may begin by suggesting how useful it would be to *you* to talk it all through. You might even be confused about who the injured party is. In response, it would be helpful to start out with some words of appreciation to them for drawing attention to their own needs as it is quite difficult for them to do so.

The difficulty with this style of attention is that it can be very passive-aggressive. The great news is that this person is capable of a very deep kind of selfless love.

3. SUCCESSFUL OR FAILED

The third style of attention goes to what is prestigious versus unimpressive. The primary desire is to be seen as successful (in money, love, art, real estate, basketball—whatever is most important to that person). The primary avoidance is to appear to have failed at anything in even the smallest way. The operative word here is "appears," as attention may not necessarily go to what is genuinely successful or failed but rather to what *appears* to be successful or failed. After all, prestige is about appearances, not substance. So there is a marked attention to status: who has it, who lacks it, whether I appear to have it or not, and so on.

When they have an issue to discuss, a person with this attention style may begin by minimizing their actual pain as it is so hard for them to acknowledge any chink in their armor. When they discuss something that upsets them, it is important to pay very close attention and allow plenty of space for the issue to develop in conversation. They may offer you opportunity after opportunity to join them in minimizing the true impact of any sorrow. It takes a big mind to avoid this—but it is worth it because eventually the small, underexpressed disappointments, frustrations, and hurts will accrue and then unexpectedly explode.

It can be especially difficult to bring up your own pain within the relationship as there is constant deflection into positivity. If you begin by recounting the genuinely successful experiences you have shared, you could then go on to share what has upset you in the name of adding to the list of accomplishments.

The difficulty with this style is that it can be quite painful to draw attention to problems, because problems indicate failure.

The good news is that this person has a preternatural capacity to remain positive and optimistic, no matter what. They have the power to uplift us and put us back in the middle of our lives with hope and inspiration.

4. SPECIAL OR ORDINARY

This is the type of person whose attention goes to how things feel—to themselves. The focus of attention is emotional content and meaning. The compass is intuition, which here means to use feeling as a guide for everything. There is a marked search for what is authentic and deep. The more intense an emotion, the more valuable it is in this search.

This person's great desire is to be seen and appreciated as special, having an unusually nuanced view into the meaning of whatever they value. While others may prize ordinariness—*I just want my life to be normal*—for this person, to be "normal" is a sign of failure. When one's avoidance is of the ordinary, there is a constant, often agitated search for what else is possible because whatever you actually see, do, or acquire immediately becomes ordinary by virtue of possessing it. So there is a kind of restlessness and push-pull in this style. This can create much confusion in love as this person is continually getting close/pulling away, getting close/pulling away.

It can be tricky to discern when this person is trying to have a painful conversation about your relationship because discussion of distress is considered a fun game. It may be challenging to gauge urgency.

To this person, deep feeling is considered a source of richness, not a problem to be solved. To approach them for a difficult conversation, it is useful to demonstrate your willingness to listen, not to a presentation on what needs fixing, but as if to a symphony, complete with movements, themes, tempo changes, crescendos, diminuendos, and so on. And, as with a concerto, if you are not familiar with the piece, you may be unsure when you are supposed to start clapping. It's important to listen through until the conclusion is unmistakable. Anything you can say in response that indicates both understanding of the actual emotional content (and please be very accurate) *and* the potential value of such feelings will deepen your connection to him or her.

The good news is that people with this attentional style are unafraid of strong feelings. They can remain powerfully present to the pain of others and will stand with you when others would run from the intensity. They can find what is genuinely poetic in every moment of life—what is beautiful, meaningful, unexpected, original. If you are looking for someone to chitchat with about your day, this is not the person to hit up. However, if you are experiencing birth, death, loss, confusion, or grief, this is the one you want by your side. They can show up for you in the peaks and valleys without ever wishing you would settle somewhere less demanding. And if you are interested in an uncommon approach to, well, *everything*, accompanied by unerring accuracy in naming the most nuanced inner states (yours or their own), you will really enjoy this person's company.

This is my personal style, and so I can speak about it from behind the lens. One of the (many, *many*) great benefits for me in understanding my attentional style is that it enables me to let myself off the hook for what I may have been told is wrong, abnormal, problematic, and so on. For example, it took me many years to realize that I was not an uncaring person/bad friend because I am not the one who loves casual phone chats or impromptu get-togethers. If that is what a person is looking for, I will not be their best friend. But when sh*t hits the fan and they need me... I am. They will have all my attention and love. I will show up in the darkest moments with infinite patience. I will never tire of hearing about the pain or cheering on the return of strength. When I say, "You can call me anytime," I really mean it... as long as you're lost in uncharted waters. When you're back on shore, don't call me anytime—because when things go back to "normal," so do I.

5. USEFUL OR USELESS

The fifth style of attention is magnetized by acquiring and stockpiling knowledge about whatever is of interest to him or her. Attention goes to systems, explanations, patterns, and reasoning, with the idea that whoever has the deepest understanding wins. A great deal of import is placed on gathering and sharing what they know. If the person with the first attentional style tells you what you are doing wrong as a sign of affection, this person tells you what they know.

Like the fourth style, the locus of attention for this person is directed inward, not outward. When you are trying to remain connected to your inner experience, everything in the outer world is seen as an interruption. To have a conversation about your relationship with this person, it is important to approach in stages as they may shut down if you drop in for a meandering chat that has not been introduced in advance. Don't drop in. Schedule the time together. Don't meander. State your agenda and, if you are feeling particularly generous, a time limitation. "I've got some new information. Do you have thirty minutes to talk about our money problems?" is better than "What's up with our money? I'm scared!"

Also like with the fourth attention style, this person is interested in what is under the surface but they have a coolness and spaciousness to their exploration that the fourth style may lack, making them ideal conversationalists who encourage you to go deeper.

The difficulty with this style is that it can be hard to know if you have actually connected. Their emotional life is not responsive to rationales and may feel strange and unknowable to them.

The gift of this attentional style is that understanding for its own sake is valued and exploring an issue does not always require attachment to an agenda. There is a natural curiosity and openness that makes conversation feel like a spacious exploration with plenty of room for questions, side trips, and general delight in the journey itself.

6. SAFE OR DANGEROUS

For this person, the focus of attention is security or danger. Because of their fine attunement to threat, people with this attentional style have an intimate relationship with doubt. "Can she really be trusted?" "Is it certain that this is what it appears to be?" "The stated policy is this, but what if they actually do that?" These questions are common in the inner life of such a person. The attunement to danger is not necessarily focused on one's self (which can, to some degree, be controlled), but on everything *except* one's self (which cannot be controlled).

To discuss your relationship with this person, it would be good to begin with an assurance of safety—but only if it is 101 percent genuine, because they can tell when you are lying (even, sometimes, when you don't know you are). "I'm not leaving you or changing the terms of our relationship, but there is something bothering me that I think we should discuss" is a good opening. Without it, they will not hear what you say because all they are listening for is the piano that is about to fall on their heads.

The difficulty here is that to introduce a problematic relationship issue could cause catastrophic thinking that frightens both of you.

The gift of this attentional style, and it is a truly remarkable one, is that once you have been established as trustworthy, you will have their attention *forever*. Loyalty and devotion are their middle names.

7. PLEASURABLE OR UNPLEASURABLE

For this person, the focus of attention is on possibilities and options. These are the people who generate a thousand ideas a minute and see opportunities wherever they look. They have a very buoyant quality and are ready to enjoy life all the time.

What could be bad, you may be wondering? Well, nothing, as long as things are going well. But once difficulty or pain enter the situation, they want to jump ship. "How can I remain focused on the horizon when you are pulling my gaze back down to earth?" is their underlying question when confronted with a problem.

It can be confusing because they are so much fun to talk with. It's not unusual to have a super-exciting, rollicking conversation with them where ideas are exchanged, plans made, and jokes told—but when you walk away, you can't quite remember if anything was actually determined. (When you always want to keep your options open, determining things is a bummer.)

To discuss your relationship can be quite tricky. Even if they are not the type to outright dismiss your pain as irrelevant, they may try to recontextualize it as a harbinger of even more goodness—which it may be, but there is also something to be said for remaining with what is painful for its own sake, and it can be very difficult to get this person to join you there. Timing for such a conversation is very important, and it's best to look for an opportunity when they are not on guard.

The good news about the person with this attentional style is they never seem to stay down for too long and are able to impart a sense of joy and hope in even the darkest situations.

8. DOMINATE OR BE DOMINATED

The eighth attentional style is fixed on power and how to possess it in any given situation. At bottom, all the attentional styles are about finding a way to feel powerful: the first type by establishing the rules, the second by making relationships with the powerful, the third by stockpiling successes, and so on. For this type of person, the attempt to acquire power is not masked in any way. It is direct, obvious, and without shame. Attention goes to how they can dominate whatever situation they are in. If they don't have the power, they will get it. If they have it, they want more. This person is always up for more and is ready to take anything—a fight, a business meeting, or an excursion to Disneyland—up a notch. Whatever you've got going on, more is better.

To discuss your relationship with this person is actually quite simple (though not easy). Basically, you've got to bonk them on the head with it. No preambles. No caveats. Neither hemming nor hawing will do because they will immediately wrest control of the conversation from you. Walking up to them out of the blue to say "Listen here, I'm miserable and I'm fixing to tell you all about it" is much, much better than "Sweetie, um, when you have time and are not too busy, could we, maybe..." Before you get to the final ellipsis, you will have been steamrolled. You just have to go for it.

The difficulty here is simply trying to match their energy. They don't often realize it, but entering a conversation with them requires a kind of forcefulness that most of us reserve for defending our home from thieves or snatching babies out of oncoming traffic. It can be exhausting.

The gift of this attentional style is their capacity for great tenderness when they love you. Because they are always so sure they are the strongest person in any situation (which they probably are), they attune to the vulnerabilities of those they care about and seek to shield them from threat.

9. COMFORTABLE OR CONFLICTUAL

The ninth attentional style could be said to comprise all of the preceding styles. This is the type of person who can truly understand a great divergence of perspectives. When you speak, they see the world through your eyes. The only perspective they cannot see is their own. This is very disorienting and actually frightening. (Imagine never being quite certain what your own point of view is.) For this style, then, attention goes to keeping the peace and remaining comfortable. As long as everyone is getting along, there is no need to declare a position on anything.

Because of the focus on remaining comfortable, it is very easy for them to lose track of their agenda (for the day, the month, their life) and there can be quite a bit of indecisiveness. For example, they may get up in the morning with only one thing to do: renew their driver's license, say. At the end of the day, they may have read a book about the history of driver's licenses, had several phone calls with friends about Department of Motor Vehicles mishaps, created a collage of past driver's license photos... but they will not have a renewed driver's license.

It is probably not hard to imagine what is difficult about discussing your relationship when one party is conflict-avoidant. I have found that being direct is rarely effective. They either run away or pretend to listen to you. If you are the kind of person who prefers to sit face to face and have a frank discussion about your issues and experiences until some conclusion is arrived at, you will have to cultivate some further communication chops. Discuss little bits at a time. Allow plenty of space for digression. And, although it sounds counterintuitive, for all their flexibility, this person can be surprisingly stubborn. Be prepared to be extremely patient.

The good news is that because this person usually does not grip their perspective too tightly, they are able to show up for the relationship in playful, creative, truly fascinating ways. They have an ability to see your point of view without filter, which is enormously loving. The job for those in a relationship with this person is to help them do so for themselves.

Three Instinctual Drives

In addition to these styles there are three instinctual drives that act as further influences on our attention: the drive for survival (self-preservation instinct), to connect with another individual (sexual, or intimate, instinct), and to become part of a group (social instinct). We all possess each of these drives, but one of them is primary for you and one—perhaps the same, perhaps not—is primary for your beloved. To have insight into these nuances is to know what you or another will find important, seek to understand, be terrified or delighted by. In other words, when it comes to relationships, it is exceptionally useful to understand this.

The person for whom the self-preservation instinct predominates will focus on issues related to survival, such as food, shelter, and money. There is a fine attunement to anything that may threaten the physical or emotional bodies.

When the sexual/intimate drive is strongest, this doesn't necessarily mean a person who wants to have sex with everyone. Rather, for this person, the focus of attention is on finding one person to connect with in every situation. The search is for one-to-one connection.

The social instinct person has different concerns altogether. The primary focus is on belonging: finding one's place in the greater world, being accepted by or leading a group. Attention is on the machinations or systems of groups.

Let's say the three instinctual drives are going to a conference. The self-preservation person will wonder: Where will I will sleep? Will it be comfortable and secure? What about the food? Will there be something there that I like? What if the room is too cold? I had better bring a sweater, not to mention snacks and my own pillow case…

The sexual drive person is not thinking about snacks. Rather, they are asking: Who will be there that I can talk to? Will there be anyone there who understands me? How will I express myself, and who will listen?

The social drive person is not thinking about snacks or specific individuals. They are wondering: Will people like me? Is this a group that will appreciate who I am? What is the seating like, and what if I'm far from the group I think I should be with? When dinner plans are made, how will I get invited to the soiree I most want to attend?

As you can see, these are three very different kinds of questions, and if you are wondering why your partner first wants to know which hotel you will stay at while your primary concern is the mission of the association, you may be caught in a conversation between someone for whom the self-preservation drive is most important and someone whose attention goes first to the social context. It is very, very helpful to know which one of these you are and which one your partner is. For example, for me, the self-preservation drive predominates. When I travel for work, say, though I hope people will like me and that I'll find a fun person to talk to, I'm too busy packing snacks and Googling photos of the hotel room to see what the bedding is like to give those other things too much thought. My husband, whose primary drive is for intimacy, is searching the attendance list to see who may be attending from his circle of acquaintance and how fun or awful it might be to encounter them.

None of the drives are preferable, obviously they are each essential, but to know which one you or your partner leads with is to be able to track the arc of attention.

Toward, Against, Away

Finally, it is useful to contemplate something called "the Hornevian directional theory," which was posited by the German psychoanalyst Karen Horney in the early twentieth century. She stated that there are three neurotic responses to threat. As with the instinctual drives, though we are each capable of all three responses, one of them is likely to predominate.

One response to danger is to move *toward* it, to pacify and mollify. The second response is to move *against* it, to remove or destroy. The third response is to move *away* from it, to avoid or ignore.

The third response, to move away, is my default reaction to danger. I am avoidant. For Duncan, it is to move against, to do battle. You have read elsewhere in this book what it is like for us to argue and how difficult it has been to find a way to fight that is useful. The directional theory explains why. When one person is rushing toward you in tackle position while the other has already found a way to disappear, there is literally no common ground to speak of, and a good fight requires a place to meet.

Once a friend asked us if we argued a lot. Simultaneously, Duncan said "almost never" and I said "all the time." Duncan thinks that arguing (which he insists on calling "discussing") is a sign that we are finally getting somewhere and could actually resolve something important. The more heated, the more important the conversation is. He likes to "have it out," which means to speak one's mind frankly and fully the moment an issue arises. Having each done so, according to this theory, the air is cleared.

To me, this method is injurious. It leaves me feeling bludgeoned, frightened, and unable to respond. I open my mouth but no words come out. All I want to do is run away. It is very disappointing to him and horrifying to me.

On those occasions when a fight is necessary, which in my world should be basically never, my preference is another tack entirely. It works like this: Each party retreats to his or her corner and thinks carefully to identify the real issue and to separate it from childhood wounds, irritations from six months ago, or having had a bad day at work. Then each crafts language to express this issue carefully, being sure to leave out anything that might be felt as an attack or insult. Finally, the parties reconvene to present their position. Each position is examined in turn until a consensus is reached.

We spent a lot of time trying to get the other to see the superiority of our arguing style. He wanted me to jump in and meet him where he was. I was never going to do this.

I needed a calmer atmosphere in which to examine whatever it was that we were arguing about. He thought this was a form of running away. For a long while, our arguments about this or that invariably included a personality critique of the other's style, which made things much worse. We became less and less able to talk and more and more afraid of encountering any type of difficulty. There was a lot of tiptoeing going on. He resented me. I was afraid of him. It sucked.

What enabled us to start viewing this as our problem (rather than as his or mine) was the Hornevian directional theory. Somehow, being able to make this distinction between toward, against, and away was very helpful. Instead of classifying him as a bully and me as disengaged, we realized that we had a simple stylistic difference. He started giving me a little more space. I experimented with jumping into the fray a little more quickly. I still hate to fight, but we do each other far less damage than we used to.

Now, mix them all together—attentional style, instinctual drive, and response to threat—and you will find a very interesting picture of yourself and your loved one.

A Note on Idiot Love

This, as you may have noticed, is a book about love—how to give it, receive it, work with it, expand it. There is much in here about what it means to open your heart and extend yourself to another in a way that is strong, genuine, and kind. I insert this note here in case you were thinking that in order to love, you have to become some kind of saint.

In his extraordinary and inscrutable body of work, the early-twentieth-century mystic philosopher George Gurdjieff helpfully described twenty-one kinds of idiots, one of which is called the "compassionate idiot." Chögyam Trungpa elaborated on this by coining the phrase "idiot compassion."

True compassion is something that arises in the moment in reaction to another being. There is no thought or agenda behind it. It is spontaneous. When someone you love tells you they have just found out their mom is sick, compassion is not a mental computation, it is an automatic arising. There is no thought of how it makes you look or whether or not it is warranted. It is simply what is happening. It is genuine.

Idiot compassion lacks this in-the-moment quality and is more about you than the object of your compassion. You may think you should be nice. You should put yourself second. You should never yell or feel disappointed. You should be understanding. Idiot compassion is about the appearance of kindness, and it is lunacy.

Somewhere along the line, many of us got the idea that love and compassion equal niceness, some kind of milquetoastiness. True love and true compassion are actually quite fierce. They are honest, direct, and pointed in that they are connected to the moment rather than to how we wish to appear. According to this definition, love and compassion may include niceness, certainly, but they are as likely to include harshness ("This is the fourth job you've lost in six months—stop being self-destructive"), withholding ("No,

I can't lend you money again because you will spend it on something weird"), or nothing ("You have not asked me what I think, so I will wait"). The only way to know which of these responses is most loving and compassionate is to let go of what you think love and compassion should look like, open your heart, and trust yourself.

4

TRUTH #4

There Is a Path to Liberation

THERE ARE WAYS to work with the truth of instability, the truth of the cause of instability, and the truth of meeting the instability together as love, and they are outlined in this chapter. They fall into three basic categories, each of which is mirrored in the sitting practice of meditation. Meditation, it turns out, is not just a path to stress reduction or heightened performance. It is a path to love.

What Meditation Has to Do with Love

One of the big misconceptions about meditation practice is that it is predicated on the capacity to observe... something. In certain practices, that something is an image that you gaze at or visualize in your mind's eye. In other practices, that object is a mantra, a sound that you chant silently or semi-audibly. Most commonly, however, the object of meditation is the breath. This is the simplest object because you are already doing it. In order to meditate with a sound or image, you introduce something that was not already there. Because we are so accustomed to directing our attention away from ourselves and onto images and/or sounds (television, games, music, chatting), the breath may seem too bare-bones, too simple. That is part of its beauty. Your breath is not a new object. You can separate from an image or a sound, but you cannot separate from your breath. Meditation on the breath is a deeply intimate situation in which we train in being with what is rather than with what we may introduce into the environment. This is very useful when it comes to loving.

As mentioned, the instruction to meditate on the breath may be interpreted to mean to observe it, which implies a sort of stepping away and looking back. However, in meditation, we don't observe the breath, we *feel* it. Just feel it. It is much harder to "feel" an image or a sound, but to feel the breath is quite natural. Feel the inhale. Feel the exhale. It is extraordinarily simple. The amount of effort required is zero because you're doing it (breathing) anyway. In meditation, you "ride" the breath with your attention and the emphasis is on *being with*. Rather than noticing yourself from a remove, you actually dissolve the remove.

Perhaps contrary to popular belief, in meditation, then, we are cultivating a relationship not with the inner observer (who can also be observed, by the way), but with the inner *feeler*—which has a lot to do with love.

First of all, we are not meditating to be good at meditation. Who cares if you are the world's preeminent feeler of the breath? Instead, we are training in present awareness. We practice being present with our breath so that when we get up from the cushion and go into our life, we can be present with that. We cultivate the ability to stay with the breath so that we can stay with our feelings, our heart, and this very moment.

Second, in the Buddhist tradition, we are not meditating to become superhumans who have transcended to another plane. We train in order to be right here, fully human, riddled with brilliance and confusion, completely vulnerable, and terrifyingly available. As it turns out, this is also the ideal mindstate for love.

So, if you want to fall in love skillfully, build a relationship that is alive and vibrant, meet the power of heartbreak (which is just about the most powerful state you can ever experience) with courage, please develop a meditation practice.

Mindfulness is often presented as a prerequisite for mastery (of leadership, art, sport, and so on). Okay, it *is* helpful in those arenas. But the real mastery is in knowing who you are, taking your seat right in the middle of your life, and finding that you are daring enough to meet it all without a shield.

The things we desire most—and I say this quite confidently even without knowing you—are the following: love (of course), wisdom, innovation, creativity, self-knowledge, and inspiration. These potent qualities all have one thing in common: they are things that we *receive*. They cannot be cranked up. No matter how brilliant your plan, you can't go out and get a breakthrough or a feeling. They have to come to you, which is much more likely when you have created space for them to do so. Meditation can be viewed as cultivating the space of receptivity. This is an exceptionally powerful thing to do. PS: Remember, do not take my word for anything. Try it yourself and see.

With an ongoing meditation practice, then, you discover that you are also practicing how to love. Your understanding of love itself will deepen in a way that is nonconceptual, nonintellectual, and *visceral*. When love appears, you will know how to recognize it. When it disappears, you will know how to work with it. When you are confused about whether love is present or absent, if you should love this person or that, or if you should stay or go, you will find that you have the ability to remain with the uncertainty on its terms and to ride it out to its organic conclusion.

The meditation technique—choosing an object of attention (precision); allowing your experience to be exactly as it is (openness); and letting go of everything to reconnect with the natural spaciousness of your mind (going beyond)—also describes the qualities we need to sustain a relationship.

Precision

In meditation, the sole object of attention is breath. Everything that is not breath is called "thinking," including thoughts, feelings, and sensations. It is that pointed. Precision is the foundation of a meditation practice, and if it is missing, you're not meditating at all. You're spacing out.

In love, the practice of precision translates into heedfulness with your words and actions—which is also known as "good manners," the importance of which cannot be overstated. Deeply good manners are rooted in thoughtfulness and considering the impact of what you say and do on others. What would a relationship be without this? Good manners could mean anything from showing up when you say you will to mentioning that you are contemplating gender reassignment. In fact, without good manners, a healthy relationship is close to impossible.

Once I was staying with my friend Crystal. After dinner, we stood at the sink talking while she washed dishes. She was elbow-deep in suds and happened to say, "I like a lot of soap." Could there be a tinier moment than this in a conversation between two people? However, since then when I've stayed at her house (which I have done a lot), I make sure to use a lot of soap when I do her dishes, whether she is there or not. This is how she likes things done, and when I am in her home I like to respect her preferences.

In my own home, I live with someone who has a place for everything. I do not have a place for everything. But I try to remember that it matters to my husband that the glasses are stacked like this and that the keys go on the hall table. I do not care about such things. He does. Here, good manners are not about doing things "his way" but about demonstrating some awareness of and respect for someone else's little preferences.

As simple as it all sounds, that is also how rare it is. This ground level of good manners may be among the most important of the qualities a person can have that make a successful relationship. True good manners are far from superficial. They are a sign that you're really paying attention to the other person and showing evidence of that in the way you act and speak. It may sound obvious to say so, but if you are with someone who doesn't care enough about you to notice you, who doesn't *think* about you, it is hard to imagine how far you could go with that person. Rather than sweeping romantic gestures or grand overtures, it is these tiny courtesies that create the foundation for the love we seek. If they are missing, the foundation will weaken over time.

Precision in a relationship also has to do with being honest and responsible about your feelings, intentions, confusions, and decisions. Honesty does not mean blurting out what you think or feel in the moment. It means telling the truth skillfully (not stupidly), presenting yourself accurately, or holding back from doing so until you are clearer about it, and, should your representations change, acknowledging that. Honesty is predicated on knowing the truth yourself, so please be very, very careful with your words and actions. Make sure they are accurate to the best of your ability.

Just as with basic thoughtfulness, basic honesty is the very foundation of a relationship. If it is questionable, love feels (and is) terrifying. Our hearts rightfully remained closed.

Openness

It is a common misconception that in order to meditate, we must "clear" the mind of thought, which is nonsense. Trying to make your mind shut up is akin to telling your ears not to hear or your eyes not to see. Your mind exists to produce thought, and getting into a tussle with it will produce a one-way ticket to Palookaville. Instead, the instruction is to allow whatever arises in your mind to simply arise, abide, and dissolve on its own while your primary attentional allegiance is to the breath. Whether your thoughts are beautiful, violent, boring, important, or silly is irrelevant. You allow them all to be as they are. Rather than trying to predetermine your experience in meditation (I need my practice to make me more patient/less stressed/a better hockey player), you open to what arises without attempting to manipulate anything. To cultivate a capacity for openness while meditating creates the capacity for openness in everything. The previous quality, precision, supports and stabilizes openness.

In a relationship, when the precision of thoughtfulness and honesty are beyond question, a strong foundation is created. This second quality, openness, arises naturally. We can afford to open up to another, so we do. The heart longs to open in this way! At this point, we become capable of understanding something quite extraordinary. You may want to sit down for this one.

The other person in your relationship is of equal importance to yourself.

I'm sort of joking (but sort of not) when I say that this came as quite a surprise to me. I had thought that finding love was going to be great for *me*. All of my attention had been on determining if this person would be good for me, if they shared my values, if they could tolerate my ineptitude and appreciate my goodness. While all of this makes sense and it is truly miraculous to find such a person, most of us tend to stop there. We see our relationship as being composed of "you" and "me." You try to meet my needs, and I try to meet yours. I make room for your foibles, you make room for mine. When we have an argument, I try to blame you and you try to blame me. When love deepens, it is because I did this and you did that. There is a constant back and forth of "you" and "me," with the emphasis on me.

I have found that this is not actually how it works. Openness isn't limited to the ability to connect with each other on the spot. It may begin there, but at some point, the continuity of openness dissolves the boundary of "you" and "me" to become "us." It is like cooking a dish with two ingredients. With the continual application of the right amount of heat, the ingredients eventually dissolve into each other to form a third thing.

Though we may enter a relationship believing it is composed of two beings (you and me), at some point this third entity (us) joins the party. Each needs care: you, me, and us. To care for one may not be the same as caring for the other. In other words, what is best for you may not serve us or vice versa. I'm not saying that "us" should always take first position, simply that in a relationship all three parties require separate but equal attention.

It was very, very difficult for me to acknowledge that I was part of an "us." I have a natural reticence about connecting with other people. I've spent my life curating independence and distance. I just feel more comfortable that way. Whether it's because I am profoundly introverted, have an avoidant attachment style (look it up—attachment theory is so interesting!), am scared of intimacy, or simply enjoy my own company, I do not know. I just know that I am parsimonious about what I give of myself. I prefer keeping to myself, and even though I may appear quite gregarious and relational (I teach, write, speak, and connect with others all day long), what I say and do is also measured to protect my sanctum sanctorum.

As mentioned earlier, after getting married and going on a honeymoon, we went back to our apartments, Duncan in Boston and me in New York City. For me, this arrangement was dreamy. When we were together, we were 100 percent focused on each other. And when we were apart, I was 100 percent focused on myself. It was awesome and I could not imagine anything better.

However, there was someone for whom this was not awesome and who could imagine something better—and that was the person I married. To discover that life was more meaningful and enjoyable to him when we were together was a bit of a shock because for me, life is more meaningful and enjoyable when I am by myself. Goodness knows what mystery of nature, nurture, and karma leads to one personality or the other, but, as our aforementioned and amazing therapist Rich explained to us, almost every couple he had ever worked with included one person who was pulling for more togetherness and one who was pulling for more separation. When he told us that both of these qualities—the wish to connect deeply and a commitment to differentiation—were necessary in a healthy relationship, something shifted and "us" was born.

Once I realized that what we each represent (him: merging; me: individuation) was important, I felt free to respect his proclivity for togetherness as a superpower rather than a threat.

The truth is, relationships seem to be beyond our capacity to grasp. They arise, abide, and dissolve under mysterious circumstances. We have no idea why we fall in love with this person and not that one. We don't know why love just disappears... and then reappears. Chemistry is inexplicable. I have no idea what causes the blissful connections and devastating ruptures that happen in my own marriage over and over. The relationship is planted somewhere just outside my capacity for understanding. The only thing I know is that I'm no longer in a relationship with a person. I'm in a relationship with a relationship. I'm not creating it. I'm taking care of it.

Once we had a fight so bad I could not stand to be in the same house with him. (It's cliché to say I can't even remember what it was about, but I can't.) I left and spent the night on the couch in my office.

I was so depressed by this argument. I dragged myself home at 6:00 a.m., dreading seeing him but also hoping I would so he could see that I remained grievously injured. As I let myself in and walked up the stairs to our bedroom, he was exiting the shower, towel around his waist. His hair was wet and smelled like drugstore pineapple. His bare chest looked kind of dewy and sweet, not at all like the chest of someone you'd hate. Although I was still angry, I could see that he no longer was. He came toward me and held his palms up to face me in an unreadable gesture. My palms spontaneously rose to mirror his—whether to stop him from coming closer or to hold him to me, I wasn't sure. However, it didn't matter which because in that moment, I realized I was caught. I couldn't push him away because our lives were no longer two separate but parallel tracks as they had been when we began living together. And I would never be able to hold him close enough to understand him. I don't know at what moment this happened, but something invisible had pushed us into a single life. We must have held each other one too many times. Inhaled each other's exhale one too many times. Had the same fight, kissed the same kiss, exchanged the same glance, eaten off the same plate, one too many times. Our bodies and hearts have formed into cutouts that can only hold the other. From this realization and from the sight of his bare chest and the scent of his pineapple hair, I softened. For whatever mysterious reason, the mere sight of him touched me so much and the only choice was to open further. Again.

Going Beyond

With the precision of thoughtfulness and honesty and the openness of dissolving the boundaries between you-me-us, something quite astonishing becomes possible: everything that transpires between you becomes an opportunity to deepen intimacy. You cease to view every moment of connection as proof of your love and each instance of distance as a problem to be solved. It all becomes part of the weave. (Not everything should be worked with in this way; see the caveat about addiction and abuse.) Rather than focusing on changing each other, you focus on knowing each other.

A few years ago, I was talking to friend of mine, a deeply accomplished practitioner and scholar in a yogic lineage.

We were discussing our formal spiritual paths and I told him that after many years of practicing this technique and that liturgy, I was no longer certain what to do in my personal practice. I had come to the end of a series of formal practices suggested by my Buddhist teacher. It felt akin to completing your undergraduate and graduate degrees and now finding yourself in the "real world" without quite knowing how to handle it. He could relate to what I was saying. He told me that his current meditation practice, which had previously consisted of a complex series of chants, visualizations, and so on, was now to simply get up in the morning, go to his cushion, and sit there. He basically tries not to do anything at all. To deepen his practice, he had discovered, there were no longer any rules to follow. And like me, he couldn't go back to following a set of instructions; nor was there a new set to jump forward into. There was only space and the feeling of groundlessness. In his tradition, he said, this stage of spiritual development is called "stupefaction." This is where no one can tell you what to do anymore. I realized that all I could do was go to the cushion and wait without knowing what I was waiting for.

I have reached a similar point in my relationship. I am stupefied. I know how to fall in love. I kind of know how to be a good partner. But maintaining a relationship over time? This is the true mystery. While there are countless movies, books, and studies about nascent stages of love and how to become an honorable partner, there is very little about *this* part of love—the depths, the point in the journey when you are in the middle of the sea, too far from shore to turn back, having found that your intended destination does not actually exist. At such a point, you have no choice but to go beyond the ideas you had about love, each other, and the journey to discover, rather than plan, the meaning of love now. And now and now and now. As the Texas band the Flatlanders wrote, "*Now it's now again*," and this is actually the best relationship guidance of all.

Now... what? Because you have cultivated precision and openness, you find that you have the courage to let go. Walls come down and you discover quite a bit of daring—the daring to open to your experience on the spot, the daring to be curious about everything rather than hopeful or fearful, and the daring to allow love to touch you whether it feels beautiful, treacherous, or dull. You slow down enough to see the ordinary magic of sharing a life with another person, of laundry and celebrations and roof repairs, of creating a world and caring for that world together. Then everything that transpires between and around you can be viewed as a chance to deepen rather than perfect love itself. It is marvelous. It is potent. However, it is not safe, never safe. Love is always coming together and falling apart.

The inability to create safety actually plots the path to true love. It's strange but true. When you work with all the chaos (and joy and sweetness and rage and so on), love becomes more than romance. It turns into something better: intimacy. Romance has got to end—that's just how it goes. But intimacy? It has no end. There is never a point where you could say, "There's no way that we could become more intimate. There's no way we can know each other more. There's no other level to get to." When it comes to creating a lasting relationship, this—intimacy, not romance—is where you want to place your chips.

Eventually you find that you are living in a kind of ambient intimacy and that it contains you, not the other way around. Rather than being in love, you live in love itself.

The Eightfold Path of Love

With precision, openness, and the willingness to go beyond, you are ready to embark on the path. What follows is a riff on the Buddha's Noble Eightfold Path, which lays out the aspects of the spiritual journey and, as it turns out, the path of love.

Right View

I'm not talking about having the right relationship strategy or holding the most evolved philosophy. Right View actually exists in the moment prior to strategies and philosophies. It has something to do with recognizing and owning the projections, judgments, hopes, and fears that most often lurk behind our strategies and philosophies.

Earlier, I spoke of the movie that plays in your head and that you project onto your environment. The closer we feel to a person, the more intense and active this movie becomes and the less likely we are to notice the actual person we purport to feel so close to.

Relatively speaking, Right View is maintaining awareness of the movie and not mistaking the human being in front of you for what you have projected onto him or her. From an absolute perspective, Right View is snapping the projector off. For good. Just take a moment and imagine what it might feel like to decommission this projector.

What would it feel like to be loved by someone who has also done so? I don't know about you, but when I think about it, I get quivers down the backbone.

Right Intention

Many, many people have declared that intention creates reality. I happen to agree. But there is a right Right Intention and wrong Right Intention, if I may. Most often, we "set" our intention to accomplish something in the material world. That is totally cool—or at least I hope it is, because I myself am riddled with ambitions and desires. But what is behind such intentions? That is the question to focus on, especially when it comes to love.

As mentioned earlier, if you were to have a look at, oh, ALL of the self-help books written about relationships, you would see that most of them are about how to get love. When we think about having love in our life, our attention most often settles on how great it would be to be loved. And you know what? It *would* be. However, this leaves 50 percent of the money on the table. It is also rather disempowering, like, I'll just sit here and hope and hope and REALLY, REALLY hope that I find love. To approach love in such a way can make you feel like a loser.

However, if we switch our intention from "I want to be loved" to "I want to love," something quite miraculous happens. We feel re-empowered. Each encounter with our fellow humans looks not like an experiment in avoiding hurt, but a vital opportunity to open up, feel what occurs within and between you, and choose something to offer from your vast storehouse of riches. Trust me—you have such a storehouse and, keep trusting me, it cannot be diminished. In Buddhist thought, as mentioned, you possess four immeasurable qualities: lovingkindness (the capacity to care), compassion (the ability to feel another's pain), sympathetic joy (the ability to feel their happiness), and equanimity (steadiness of heart). So you can afford to experiment (skillfully, wakefully, intelligently) with the intention of giving from the heart.

Right Speech

When speech arises from Right View and Right Intention, the probability that it will be a channel for greater intimacy is vastly increased.

Right Speech in relationships could be the topic of a book itself. So much depends on how, when, and why we address each other and, beyond this, how capable we are of listening clearly and responding accurately.

Right Speech is composed of three things:

No lying. Of course you don't want to make things up or be misleading to any degree. Anyone with the intention to love truly would agree. But it is not that simple. In order to avoid lying, we first have to know the truth of what we think and feel. That takes tremendous precision and courage. So begin by being brave and not lying to yourself.

No divisive speech. Pretty much every argument I have ever had with my partner has been based on divisive speech. When I try to blame or hurt him, I am dividing myself from him. It is quite a trick to argue with full-on heat and volume (nothing wrong with that) and remain connected, side by side, at the same time.

No idle speech. Basically this means that if you don't have anything to say, don't talk. I'm not saying that all chitchat is a bad idea—but are you using your speech as a kind of sweet ambient background noise (which is awesome) or because you are bored and looking for a way to entertain yourself?

Right Speech in the positive would be: be truthful; use words to bridge the gap; and let your speech have a purpose.

None of this is easy. When people talk about how hard relationships are and how much work they take, they are most often referring to the difficulty of Right Speech. This is because relationships are not for babies. It takes a very big mind and heart, not to mention tremendous clarity, to use speech to benefit and delight.

Right Action

This means being a decent person all the time, not just when someone is watching. In Buddhism, Right Action covers all forms of non-harming, such as don't kill, don't steal, don't lie, don't be sexually (or emotionally) abusive, and don't be an addict. Don't be a dick, is how I think of it.

Right Action does not mean eschewing these things when we might get caught. It means eschewing them all the time.

In relationships, non-harming is very tricky. We usually don't mean to hurt the one we love, but we find that we do so in all sorts of ways, big and small. Like, every day. You could begin by recognizing your own pain. There is no such thing as hurting others without first being in pain yourself. Don't let things fester. Clean up your messes. This doesn't mean sweep your emotional pains and sorrows under the rug or throw them out—rather, do your inner housekeeping and be assiduous about it. When you feel angry or hurt, work with it. A lot rides on keeping your inner environment well lit.

In Tibetan Buddhism, there is a practice called *lojong* or "mind training." It presents fifty-nine slogans to contemplate and one of them, "Drive All Blames into One," provides a great summation of Right Action. It does not mean blaming yourself for everything. It means taking responsibility for everything as if you had caused it to happen—but not hurting yourself by chastising, shaming, or being aggressive toward yourself. Just get to work on whatever has just happened. Then the ability to avoid hurting others by chastising, shaming, or being aggressive toward them is a thousand times stronger.

Right Household (Right Livelihood)

The next step along the Buddhist Eightfold Path is Right Livelihood. This refers to the work you do to gain resources on which to base your life. For our purpose, I've reframed this as "Right Household," meaning what we often create as a basis for relationships—a home or some kind of shared space. Just as Right Livelihood includes some very straightforward parameters about not earning money from killing, poisoning, or stealing from others, Right Household is similarly straightforward. Don't live in a mess. Don't spend more than you have. Share responsibilities consciously. Be cognizant of not being the only person in the house (or apartment, room, car... wherever you spend most of your time together) and attend to the environment accordingly. The space you share is the environment in which your relationship transpires. The more conscious (but not in a silly way) you can be about the space around you, the fewer obstacles you will find between you.

Right Effort

Right Effort means continually working to apply Right View, Intention, Speech, Action, and Household. Even when you're tired. Grumpy. In love. Mad. Bored. Ecstatic. Always! It means not giving up on deepening your capacity to love and be loved. (Until and unless you determine that giving up is the right thing to do. Then do not give up on giving up.)

Right Mindfulness

Once, Chögyam Trungpa showed his students a picture of a cloud. *What is this picture of?* he asked. *A cloud*, they answered. *No*, he said. *It is a picture of the sky.*

Without the sky, the cloud would just be a puff. Without the cloud, the sky would be an empty space. Foreground and background are inseparable, and it is very helpful to acknowledge that the space around you informs what arises within it and that what arises within it informs the space.

When it comes to love, being aware of both foreground and background means being cognizant of what you feel and what your partner may be experiencing as well. But it also means attending to the ambient qualities of the environment you inhabit together. This is a very mysterious thing to do. Sometimes I walk into our house and it feels warm and bright. Other times, it feels heavy and stuck. I may be in possession of a good mood right now, but my partner is crabby (or vice versa). I feel his mood and it changes things: my thoughts, hopes, fears, and energy. Right Mindfulness is a dance of awareness that swirls among all these things: you, me, the space we are in, and the way it all changes moment to moment. Like a kaleidoscope, each time one cell rotates, the entire pattern shifts. If you can roll with this for even five minutes, you will learn a lot.

Right Absorption

To be absorbed is to stabilize two qualities of mind: mindfulness and awareness. Mindfulness means precise attention to the present. Awareness is attunement to insight, wisdom, feelings, sensations, and what lies beyond such things. Right Absorption means not becoming distracted by discursive or conceptual thoughts. This doesn't mean you don't have discursiveness or conceptuality. It simply means that rather than resting with them, you rest in mindfulness-awareness, which are inseparable from each other.

Right Absorption brings us back to Right View: the willingness to step beyond conventional thought to be with what is. When we can attend to our beloved, our self, and the present moment, we find that we reside in love itself.

The Warrior (in Love)

I practice in the Shambhala Buddhist lineage (a Tibetan tradition). One of the very first things that attracted me to it was its teachings on what is called "spiritual warriorship." The warrior's weapons are gentleness and fierceness. Strong emotion is seen not as an obstacle, as it may be in other traditions, but as a potent source of power. To work with emotion as a source of wisdom, you cultivate a state of fearlessness, beginning with your fears about yourself. A warrior, taught Chögyam Trungpa, is first and foremost one who is not afraid of herself and is willing to experience fear head on. Since the primary obstacle to loving and being loved seems to be fear, it is useful to examine how one might go beyond it.

You may wish I wouldn't say this again, but that way is to have a meditation practice. When we sit with ourselves as we are, we encounter all kinds of things, including our brilliance, confusion, rage, and silliness. No matter what, the instruction is always the same. Stay. Allow. Be with. *Look*. As it turns out, when you know how to stop, turn around, and look directly at yourself, you come into possession of a superpower. It is called kindness. Rather than protecting yourself at every turn by clinging to, blaming, or ignoring who you are, you can actually be right there, present and accounted for.

It is a strange karmic trick that at those times when we most want to harden our hearts and ignore others, what is called for is to soften, first to ourselves and then to everyone else.

In recent years, there has been a lot of glory heaped on the quality of vulnerability, and rightfully so. (Thanks, Brené Brown and others!) Vulnerability is the gateway to what we desire most: love, wisdom, creativity, insight, and so on—none of which are possible when we are trapped by our conceptuality: opinions, judgments, hopes, fears, and ideas. To feel something fresh, discover something new, attune accurately to the present moment, we have to let go of it all. This is what vulnerability means: living without the protective armor of preconceived notions. This is a very scary thing to do; hence, vulnerability is associated with feeling awkward and unbalanced. It is also an exceptionally courageous thing to do, to go into the world unarmored by your stories.

Vulnerability is the prerequisite for love. What is the prerequisite for vulnerability? Uncertainty. What is the last thing we want to feel in our relationships? Uncertainty. It takes so much gumption to not know—far, far more than it does to hold a multitude of assertions, no matter how carefully constructed. To enter this most powerful arena where everything is at stake, wide awake, with your heart open, unarmed by concepts, is to take the warrior's stance. Rather than holding a thousand lists and road maps in her hands, the warrior meets love alone and bare-handed. Her weapons are the gentleness of opening to what is and fierceness of allowing herself to feel. She is responsive. Alive. Ready to risk everything because risking everything is the only option. She is unafraid of fear and is willing to be as foolish, luminous, chaotic, and brilliant as she really is, without shame. It turns out that this is what is meant by a state of grace: to be fully one's self. Then, when love is offered or received, it is true love.

This brings us back to where we started, with Chögyam Trungpa's astonishing words: "The only true elegance is vulnerability." My sincere wish is that these words have taken on new meaning for you and have planted within your heart the seeds of true love.

5

PRACTICES TO REMAIN CONNECTED

IT IS ONE thing to read a lot of ideas about what makes relationships work and it is another thing to bring these ideas into your experience. We live in a very heady world. We mistake an excellent rationale for accomplishment of that rationale. Articles about meditation, for example, often focus on its many scientifically proven benefits. It is interesting to learn about those. However, understanding why meditation works is not the same thing as actually meditating. No matter how much research you have done and how convinced you are that meditation is awesome, when you sit down on the cushion, all of that fades away and you are faced with the reality of just doing it. When something cool happens, you may think, *That research is spot on and I am really doing this!* and miss the simplicity and directness of your positive experience to jump right to delighting in the correctness of your judgment. Conversely, when something boring or sad happens, we miss that too and instead put an X in the "This Works" column.

We spend an awful lot of time checking our experience, not for its content, but for proof or disproof of what we already believe. While it is great to check your assumptions, correct assumptions do not equate with accomplishing anything, just as incorrect assumptions do not correlate with accomplishing nothing.

All of this goes to say that while I hope you have enjoyed reading my thoughts on Buddhism, love, and relationships, it is not enough to choose what you agree or disagree with and think that either will help you to deepen your relationships and capacity to love. No theory will enable you to open your heart. No assumption will protect you from heartbreak. No strategy will cause you to find true love. I'm sorry. When the heart opens, shatters, or is dazed, all thoughts vaporize and you are left with your emotions, longings, and the consequences of karma. To become overly enamored of theories creates a lot of kooky diversions when, really, all you can do is feel. Pay attention. Lean in.

Falling in love, sustaining love, and losing love are all very complex and powerful and, more often than not, catch us unaware. Yet, without having any way to predict what will happen, we can still practice being prepared for what may come. This is what spiritual practices do. They prepare us to meet our experience head on while offering no guarantee about what that experience might be.

These following three practices help keep our hearts open, pliant, and strong.

Breath-Awareness Meditation

Mindfulness is the ability to place your attention on what you would like to place it on and then hold it there. This is becoming increasingly difficult in our culture, in which a billion things per second are calling for that attention. Our attention is now more accustomed to jumping and bouncing and becoming exhausted than it is to resting on an object of our choosing. The consequence of this is that we may look at the person we love but find that we are incapable of actually hearing them. Being unable to slow down enough to take each other in becomes very problematic and even unloving. Love begins with giving our attention to our beloved, which also means dropping our attention on ourselves, at least for a time. It continues by remaining willing to give your attention to this person during times of concord and discord. If you think about it, the relationship is over when you are no longer willing to give your attention to the other person at all. Of course, many people stay together anyway, sort of tolerating each other while placing as little attention as possible on the partner while hoping to gain as much attention as possible from him or her. This is my personal definition of relationship hell. But if you are unwilling to pay attention to someone or, worse, resent having to do so—or if your partner feels this way about you—the relationship can find no purchase. Attention is the vehicle, the journey, and the destination all rolled up into one.

There is no difference between love and your ability, your willingness, your courage to place your attention on this other person who is so important and has so much power to hurt you. When you can do so without an agenda to actually hear them, take them in, feel them in your heart... this is love.

Usually when we listen to the person we're in a relationship with—and the closer we are, the more this seems to happen—the less we hear them and the more we hear the hopes and fears that are evoked by them. So we're actually not even relating to them. We're relating more to what we hope and pray will happen or are terrified may happen. So mindfulness is not just a stress reduction technique or a relaxation thing. It's actually a form of courage: it's you saying to the person you love: *I will let my attention on myself go for now so that I can feel and hear and see you*... and then seeing what happens next. The way to cultivate this skill is by learning to meditate.

How to Meditate

Find a comfortable place to sit. You can sit on a meditation cushion or in chair. Both are fine.

If you and your partner want to practice together, figure out a time and place that is convenient for both of you. Keep it simple. Create a spot that you feel good about returning to.

It's also totally fine to meditate on your own. Personally, I prefer to practice by myself. Keep it simple. Create a spot that you feel good about returning to.

Before you begin, take a moment to reconnect with a sense of openness and stability by remembering the spaciousness of the sky above you and the richness of the earth below. Then acknowledge to yourself that this is your time to meditate (rather than to think through problems or add to your to-do list) and that you will devote yourself to it wholeheartedly. Don't phone it in. Commit.

Set a timer for five, ten, or twenty minutes, whatever feels right to you. When it comes to meditation, consistency is more valuable than duration. Five minutes a day seven days a week is better than thirty-five minutes one day a week.

There are three things to be mindful of in meditation practice.

BODY

The practice begins as you take your seat. Feel yourself sitting on the cushion or chair and really give your weight to it. Land. Then check to make sure you're sitting up straight—not like someone who is trying to boast of good posture, more like someone who is unashamed to be exactly who they are: a good human being who is just sitting there breathing. Feel your body breathing. Your posture should be firm but also supple.

If you are seated on a cushion, cross your legs loosely in front of you. Some people prefer to have their knees lower than the hips, some higher. Play around and see which one works for you. You may have to experiment with cushion heights to find the right setup for yourself.

If you are on a chair, sit with your feet are flat on the floor. If you are under about five foot ten, you will probably feel more comfortable if you put a cushion under your feet.

Place your hands, palms down, just above your knees or at mid-thigh. Let your shoulders and belly relax. The biceps should be parallel with the torso.

Tuck your chin a little bit so that the back of the neck is long and the chin is parallel with the ground. Your mouth is closed but let the lips be slightly parted, tongue resting on the roof of the mouth. Let the jaw relax.

The eyes remain open. The gaze is soft and cast slightly down, to a spot about six to eight feet (around one and a half meters) in front of you. Don't stare at that spot; simply let your gaze rest there.

BREATH

Place attention on your breath. Feel the rise and fall of your body as it breathes. Feeling is different than observing or thinking about breath. To observe implies a kind of stepping away and looking back at yourself. To feel means to be with. This is about being with.

MIND

Of course, your mind will continue to make thoughts because that is what it does. In none of my research have I come across the instruction "Tell yourself to shut up" as part of meditation practice. Trying to make your mind stop thinking is like trying to make your eyes stop seeing or your ears stop hearing—very frustrating and also not the point. Instead, when thoughts arise, you simply notice them and allow them to float by. Keep your attention on your breath. Most of your thoughts will come and go without really distracting you from your breath.

However, sometimes you may notice that you are so absorbed in thought that you have forgotten about your breath altogether. Yay! Far from being a problem, this is wonderful. You just woke up. You saw where you were. With this awareness, you have choices. Without it, you have none. The choice here is to say to yourself, when you notice that you've departed fully from breath, "thinking." Label that moment what it is: thinking. Then gently let go of the thought. It doesn't matter if it is beautiful, horrifying, important, trivial, violent, powerful, or silly. Just let go. And, also gently, return attention to breath. Take a fresh start. The number of fresh starts you are allowed in any given meditation session is infinite.

Mindfulness of body can create a sense of stability. Mindfulness of breath creates a sense of peace. And mindfulness of mind creates a sense of tremendous spaciousness. Together, mindfulness of body, breath, and mind establish your meditation practice.

For continued support for your meditation practice, please join the Open Heart Project, my online meditation community. It's free and I'll send you a guided ten-minute meditation video every week: susanpiver.com/open-heart-project.

Lovingkindness Meditation

As mentioned in the beginning of this book, at one point in our early marriage, we hit one of those awful skids.

One day I was madly in love with him and saw both his strengths and weaknesses as adorable, but the next all I wanted was to get away from him. It was like reaching for my eyeglasses in the morning to discover that the lenses had turned black overnight. There was no segue from Mr. Wonderful to Mr. Get-Off-of-Me, but there he was all the same. Why did my heart close up? *I have no idea.* Some combination, perhaps, of triggered childhood wounds, basic human grumpiness, hormonal chaos, not getting enough sleep, and being hangry. No one actually knows why these things happen. Honestly, if anyone purports to explain to you the rhythms of your own heart, please take a few steps back. Psychologists, neurobiologists, ministers, and talk-show hosts are working around the clock to figure out the systems that govern love, but there are no such systems. It is a mystery. Thank goodness.

We explored various theories about what was plaguing us, but we couldn't figure it out. There was nothing to point to; everything seemed pretty much like it did the day before with one big difference: we just didn't like each other anymore. The chasm widened and a dark heaviness settled over our lives. I was scared. It was like we were in separate rowboats drifting away in opposite directions while we looked imploringly at each other. Very strange.

As you now know me to do, I began thinking about the Buddhist teachings and how they might help us. I remembered this from Chögyam Trunpga:

"Relative bodhichitta (lovingkindness) comes from the simple and basic experience of realizing that you could have a tender heart in any situation."

In any situation. So, I didn't have to be pleased, contented, and happy to offer love. I could be disgruntled, cranky, and coldhearted—which was really great news at this particular moment. Further into my Buddhist studies, I learned that love does not necessarily have anything to do with what you feel and is more about how you act. The formal practice of lovingkindness is just such an action.

Lovingkindness meditation (*metta* in Pali, *maitri* in Sanskrit) is more than 2,500 years old. It is said to have been introduced by the Buddha to a cohort of monks who had been attempting to meditate in the forest in close proximity to where he was teaching. This particular spot turned out to be unworkable. The existing denizens were not exactly welcoming. They felt that their space had been invaded (and it had) and did everything they could think of to drive the monks out. They made loud noises. They made a horrible stench. They appeared as scary apparitions. None of these are particularly easy situations in which to maintain meditative equipoise. When the monks turned to the Buddha for advice, they expected, I imagine, to be directed to a new locale. Instead, they were directed to return to the original location and practice lovingkindness. When they did, not only did the original inhabitants stop terrorizing them, they actually became the monks' protectors. That is how powerful this practice is. It can turn enemies into friends.

When it comes to relationships, you may be all too familiar with this story. You move in with your love and find that they do indeed make loud noises and horrible stenches, and can scare the living daylights out of you from time to time. It is common to feel that the other does not know how to make space for you or, if they try, they do it in the wrong way. You may think you are making space for each other, but really you're just creating the kind of space you want to live in and then hoping that your partner falls into line. To share space, whether it is the space of a car on a long drive or a shared home, is fraught with big and small expectations, hopes, and fears. In fact, when it comes to making a relationship work, figuring a way to inhabit space together becomes more important than figuring out if you love each other. In the "love affair" phase, feelings are everything. In the "relationship" phase, feelings are fuel and fodder, to be sure, but space, time, and belongings are the way it all manifests. Just like with the irate denizens, when it comes to relationships, we can feel we have been encroached upon in ways for which we had not given permission. At such a point, lovingkindness practice is what you want.

I want to offer you two versions of lovingkindness meditation: traditional and nontraditional.

Traditional

The practice of lovingkindness begins with yourself. This is a very important step. Don't gloss over it. If you can't find a way to feel tenderness toward yourself, the rest of the practice won't work.

Parenthetically, I imagine that 2,500 years ago, the idea of feeling kindly toward yourself wasn't such a big deal. However, in our day, this might be the most difficult part of the practice. We are so incredibly hard on ourselves. Most of us offer kindness toward ourselves begrudgingly and then only after we've accomplished some super human task and feel we "deserve" it. But you can soften to yourself much more than this. In fact, extending the hand of friendship to yourself is crucial, not just for your love life, but for every aspect of your life.

STEP ONE

To begin the practice, sit or lie down somewhere comfortable. Close your eyes. Take a few minutes to settle down by focusing on your breath until you feel that you're actually there. Then bring to mind a sense of how hard you have worked in your life to find love and happiness. You have done your best and sometimes this has resulted in happiness, sometimes in sorrow. Either way, your intention was to find happiness, joy, and contentment. You know this is true, deep down in your heart. Let respect and appreciation for yourself wash over you. From within these feelings, send yourself the following wishes:

May I be happy.
May I be healthy.
May I be peaceful.
May I live with ease.

These phrases are traditional, but you are welcome to alter them to make them feel more natural. Spend a while (a few minutes or so) wishing these things for yourself, as ardently as you can.

STEP TWO

Next, bring to mind a loved one—someone who, when you just think of them even for a second, causes your heart to soften. It could be a relative, friend, child, or pet. Take in what you know of their efforts to find love and happiness and how they have had gains and losses. Recall your own feelings of joy, satisfaction, sadness, rage, and numbness, and know that this loved one has felt or will feel these exact same things. You would do anything to take some of their burden on, and, through this practice, you can. Feeling your love for them, send them the phrases for a while.

May you be happy.
May you be healthy.
May you be peaceful.
May you live with ease.

STEP THREE

The next step is to think of someone called "the stranger." This is someone you know but don't have any feelings about. Maybe a person you pass on the street all the time or the waitress who brought you lunch. You can assume beyond doubt that they are just like you and your loved one—trying hard, meeting with successes, meeting with failures. They have felt or will feel exactly as you and your loved one. This is true for all beings, period. Without even knowing them, you can offer your loving kindness.

May you be happy.
May you be healthy.
May you be peaceful.
May you live with ease.

STEP FOUR

Next comes the really interesting part. The fourth step in the instruction is to choose someone called "the enemy." This is someone who has harmed you. Someone you don't like. Someone who you believe has done wrong with a capital W. No matter how much you despise them, you can also know that, even though it may look insane to you, they too are actually trying to find happiness. Think that, regardless of how they got there, whether or not they "deserve" it, this enemy has longed to be loved and has also felt the sharp, seemingly unendurable pain of loss. In their own way, they have felt what you have, exactly. Without excusing their behavior, you can still wish for them the following:

May you be happy.
May you be healthy.
May you be peaceful.
May you live with ease.

STEP FIVE

End the practice by sending your loving kindness to all beings who seek to love and be loved. Open your heart to the knowledge that, at one time or another, or even right now, all beings have experienced longing, sorrow, loss, egregious injustice, and so on. You can do it. Your heart is definitely that big. Holding this understanding of the shared community of beings who have wished so deeply for love and happiness, extend the following:

May all beings be happy.
May all beings be healthy.
May all beings be peaceful.
May all beings live with ease.

Then, when you're ready, let the entire practice go and sit quietly for a few minutes.

Nontraditional

You can do this practice for and with your partner by following the exact same steps. Begin by offering loving kindness to yourself and end by offering it to all beings, but place your partner in the three intermediate positions as loved one, stranger, and enemy.

STEP ONE

Offer loving kindness to yourself as described above.

STEP TWO

Place your partner in the position of loved one. Whether or not you feel that love in this particular moment, please look at him or her through the eyes of love. See him or her in their most lovable aspect. Remember what is so special and compelling about this amazing person. When you can see him or her in this way, wish the following:

May you be happy.
May you be healthy.
May you be peaceful.
May you know love.

STEP THREE

Place your partner in the position of stranger. No matter how well you may know each other, there are parts of this person that you do not know and will never know. We are all deeply mysterious creatures. Fix this person's face in mind as someone you don't know. See him or her as if for the first time, not knowing anything about them. Wish for your loved-one-as-stranger the following:

May you be happy.
May you be healthy in body and mind.
May you be peaceful.
May you know love.

STEP FOUR

Then move on to seeing your loved one in his or her manifestation as an enemy. There are things about this person that drive you crazy, cause you suffering, confound you entirely. To see him or her as an enemy does not mean to focus on everything you don't like about him or her. Rather, it means to connect with what is most wounded and hidden about your loved one and that therefore causes him or her to act in ways that hurt you (and him- or herself). Bring to mind your loved one in his or her most vulnerable and confused aspects. Feel, really feel, how much he or she hurts, irritates, or misunderstands you due to these wounds. Don't get all wishy-washy. You can feel as pissed off or disgruntled as you like. Still, you can wish for him or her as your enemy:

May you be happy.
May you be healthy in body and mind.
May you be peaceful.
May you know love.

STEP FIVE

Finally, offer loving kindness to the entirety of who your partner is—lovable, inscrutable, and infuriating. Sit quietly for a few minutes or longer before heading back into your life.

To close the practice, look at each other for a few moments. Look at your partner's face, see them through the eyes of love. Take that aspect of them in. Next, look at them as a stranger. This is also true. There are parts of them that you do not and will never know. Then, look them as an "enemy," meaning as someone who has developed difficult qualities that are rooted in pain suffered in the past. In the last moments, allow all of these aspects to blend. Your partner is a loved one, a stranger, and an enemy. Spend the final moments gazing at him or her in total. This closing step could take thirty seconds or you could spend longer if you like. (Although, personally, I would find anything greater than a minute to be excruciating. I'm shy like that.) Give each other a hug and, as you do, feel that you hold in your arms a creature of astonishing, beautiful, confounding mystery. Then let go.

Doing this practice may or may not be difficult. If it raises feelings of grief, rage, confusion, impatience, hang in there. Do not try to push these feelings away. Let them in. Try to feel them without—and this is the most important thing ever—judging yourself or the meaning of your feelings. Just feel. If you laugh, cry, or fume, it's okay. As you cycle through the stations of this practice—self, loved one, stranger, enemy, all beings—know deep in your heart that what you feel is also felt by each of these beings, including your partner, no more, no less. They have suffered what you suffer, definitely. Thus wishing them loving kindness and wishing it for yourself become entwined.

This, the nontraditional practice of lovingkindness, is how I resolved my disconnect with Duncan, the one mentioned at the start of this section. I sat in front of my shrine with the intention to practice lovingkindness in the traditional sense. My first thought was to place Duncan in the role of loved one. That felt ingenuine. Stranger? Sure, I had no idea who he had turned into. Enemy? Yes, I felt that we were quite clearly in opposition to one another. Since

I could not choose from between these roles, I assigned to him each role. When I practiced lovingkindness for him as my loved one, it's not that I remembered all his good qualities—it's more that my heart simply and wordlessly softened. When I held him in my heart as a stranger, I realized that there were parts of him I would never know, and I found this to be intriguing. As my enemy, I gave free rein to my fears that he was not the right person for me and that we would continually disappoint each other. Though this was not pleasant, I realized that rather than being upset with him, I was *scared*. While anger is harsh and displaced onto someone else, fear is more workable and brings a greater sense of agency.

When he came home that night, nothing had really changed between us. But when he walked in the door, I smiled. When we embraced hello, he smelled good, dear, like *him*. He put on some music. We sat on the couch. The environment, rather than menacing, seemed warm. The door to love had somehow reopened. Was this the result of my lovingkindness practice? I didn't really know. I was just glad that whatever had gotten a hold of us had let go.

The Practice of Conversation

The idea that talking to your loved one can be a spiritual practice may sound silly. I mean, you talk to each other all day long. Sure, okay. But if you're anything like me and my partner, conversations always seem to have a specific purpose. We talk about what to eat for dinner. We exchange information about our home. We share stories about our day, childhood, and dreams about the future. We whisper words of love when we're happy and yell at each other when we're angry. All well and good. The conversation practice described below has no particular purpose beyond connecting with each other in a spacious, agendaless way.

This practice takes about fifteen minutes. You could do it every day, or on those days when you have a little time to spare. (I know everyone is really busy.) When you wake up, come home from work or school, or before you go to sleep are great times. You can do this practice when you're really happy with each other, in a huge fight, or ensnared by ennui. It is not without its perils, but it can apply to basically every situation I can think of.

This practice comes out of a group exercise called "dyad work," which is basically when two people talk to each other in response to a given question. The question I propose for this practice is very simple. It is the following:

How are you?

The rules of the dyad are as follows:

Each person is given an allotted time to speak. (Five minutes is good.)

The person who is speaking owns that five minutes, meaning he or she has the floor.

The listener is not expected to respond at all, rather to give his or her attention to the speaker fully. Since the listener does not have to answer, diagnose, analyze, or fix, he or she can afford to simply listen intently with the sole intention of hearing what their partner is saying. Cross-talk is disallowed. No matter how much you want to say something in reaction, whether it is meant to be helpful, hurtful, defensive, or loving, don't. Just listen.

As the listener, you could even keep nonverbal responses to a minimum. Don't stare blankly at your partner, but do give him or her space without too much nodding, head shaking, glaring, or gesturing. Your responses are your business for now, not your partner's.

Use a timer. When it signals the end of the first talking-listening period, the speaker can wrap up his or her final thought but add no more to the conversation.

The listener says two words to conclude: "thank" and "you."

Then switch; repeat.

To begin, set aside time during which you and your partner will not be disturbed. Turn off all devices: phones, computers, tablets, television. Relish the dimming of inputs and feel yourself protected from disturbances, not reachable by the world.

Set the timer for two minutes and sit together comfortably in meditation. Decide who will speak first. The listener sets the timer for five minutes. When the opening tone is heard, the listener asks, "How are you?" The speaker answers this question in whatever way they wish. They can talk about their day, mention aches and pains, talk about emotions, disclose concerns—whatever they like. If the speaker runs out of things to say, just sit quietly together. No prompting or "helping."

It is important for the speaker to avoid using this time for the "airing of grievances." This is a time to speak about yourself and, well, how you are doing. I know that couples can carry around a lot of unaired grievances and, given the chance when you know your partner won't sass back, may take advantage of this moment to hurt the other whether in small or big ways. This is to be avoided. If you are hurt or angry about something, share that. "I feel hurt by something you said yesterday (or five years ago) and a big part of me is working on coming to terms with that" is different from "How am I? I'll tell you how I am. What you said yesterday (or five years ago) was insulting and ridiculous. I'm pissed." "I'm pissed" is actually fine, but the rest of this sentiment includes blaming and baiting and is not fine. Return again and again to the question: "How am I?" If you asked me how I was and I replied, "You're insulting and ridiculous," I would not exactly be answering your question. I would be talking about you, not me. Keep the focus on the latter.

If you hear your partner breaking a rule of dyad practice, you're going to have to deal with it. In the midst of the dyad is not a time to correct or dismantle the interaction. Such a conversation will have to wait.

As the listener, you may hear things you'd like to comment on when it's your turn. Please try to avoid making lists and rehearsing counterpoints. Remember, your sole responsibility here is to listen and grasp what is being said not according to your logic, but according to your partner's. When it is your turn, you may disclose feeling hurt, angry, or misunderstood if you would like. Just as in meditation when you let thoughts and feelings go to return attention to breath, in conversation let them go to return attention to your partner's words. This is the key to making this practice meditative rather than psychological or legalistic.

Again, when the speaker is done, say "thank you." That is all. Then reverse roles.

When the second five-minute period is up, immediately return to a short sitting meditation, say, two minutes. In this way, the practice of conversation is bracketed by very short breath-awareness practice sessions.

To end conversation practice, conclude the second short sitting by inviting love to continue blossoming. I like to say (silently) something like this:

May I live in love.

May my partner live in love.

May all beings live in love.

May this relationship flourish.

You are free to change these words so that they are more resonant for you, but the basic progression is me–you–everyone–us. The only instruction is this: Keep it simple.

These practices—of meditation, lovingkindness, and conversation—are most useful when done with some consistency. These practices are not to be seen as devices particularly, but as a way to spend time together. They build connection into everyday life in a way that is simpler than date nights or vacations. Then, when you do go on a date or take a vacation, you won't have to rebuild your connection to each other because you have intentionally visited with it every day. This practice is about "doing" connection rather than studying it or talking about it.

6

LOVING YOU MORE THAN US

WHEN I WAS a teenager, I lived by myself overseas. I fell in love with a really wonderful man, also a teenager. We lived together with much happiness. The love we shared was beyond what might be expected between two kids. It was piercing. It was healing. It was joyous. After about a year, though, I began to question the direction of my life. Was this it for me, to live in this foreign country and stay with this one man for the rest of my life? I was at a crossroads that had nothing to do with my love for him (which was immense) but everything to do with the vision I had for my life. We talked about it endlessly. Should we stay together or split up? We would lie on our bed at night and hold each other and cry. I couldn't imagine parting but neither could I imagine making such lasting life choices at this young age. What to do, what to do?

One night he told me he thought I should return home to fulfill my destiny. I knew he loved me and did not want us to part—What made him say this? I wondered. "I love you more than I love us" was his explanation.

This was an extraordinary display of what it means to seek to give rather than receive love. The way he said it, "I love you more than I love us," gave me a formula for all the relationships that followed. This lesson delivered many years ago to a seventeen-year-old girl by a nineteen-year-old boy taught me what to choose in a relationship besides my own comfort. He taught me to choose love itself.

There is a place where giving and receiving love become indistinguishable, where you, me, and us blend. That place is reached when you stop imagining that love is a feeling and begin to think of it as a gesture or a way of holding your mind.

APPENDIX A

How to Establish a Home Meditation Practice

I HEARTILY INVITE YOU to join my online meditation community, the Open Heart Project, for free weekly guided meditations. There are many other wonderful books, videos, and apps that can help you to establish a practice. My favorites are suggested in Appendix B. No matter what you choose to practice, the following suggestions can be useful.

Be reasonable. Set a very doable goal. Don't say, for example, "For the rest of my life, I will meditate every single day for thirty minutes." The first time you miss a day, you'll feel terrible. Instead, establish something like this: "Starting tomorrow, I will meditate Monday through Friday, for ten minutes a day. For two weeks." Whatever you decide, stick with it, and at the end, reassess.

Be consistent. Consistency is more important than duration. Ten minutes a day five days a week is better than fifty minutes one day a week. Try to practice at the same time each day. You may need to experiment to determine that time. Most people like to practice in the morning, but if you're a night owl, you may do better later in the day.

Straighten up. Posture is important, and not just because sitting up straight enables energy to flow properly within the body. We want to avoid pain. That said, it's not at all unusual to be mildly uncomfortable in the first days or weeks of practice. It can take a while for your body to adjust to sitting in this way and in the meantime, your foot may fall asleep or you could feel a little achy in your joints. Don't worry, these will pass. Of course, if the pain is more than mild, you need to pay attention to this! If you're sitting on the floor, move to a chair. Make adjustments to your posture to avoid injury.

Connect. If you decide you want to make meditation a part of your life, that is fantastic. In this case, it is very important to establish a relationship with a meditation instructor, which just means someone who has been practicing for longer than you and who is connected to a lineage you resonate with. In my tradition, Shambhala Buddhism, you can go to a Shambhala center in your town and request such an instructor. It is free and we have all had the same training. It's so good to have someone to talk with. You could also find support at a Zen or Vipassana center. The thing is to find someplace connected with lineage—no New Age stuff. It is also recommended to practice with others from time to time. It's great to practice at home alone, but it deepens your experience to sit with others.

Practice and study. Study and practice. They say that practice and study are like two wheels on a cart. With only one wheel, a cart just goes in circles. So while it's very important to actually practice meditation, it's as important to understand the underlying point of view. Most of us lean toward either study or practice. So if you prefer "study" (that is, learning about meditation), add some doing to the mix. If you prefer doing, add in some learning. It's as simple as reading a few pages from a book about meditation before you sit.

APPENDIX B

Suggested Readings

Pema Chödrön, *The Wisdom of No Escape and the Path of Loving-Kindness* (Shambhala, 2010).

Eli Jaxon-Bear, *From Fixation to Freedom: The Enneagram of Liberation* (Leela Foundation, 2001).

Sakyong Mipham, *The Lost Art of Good Conversation: A Mindful Way to Connect with Others and Enrich Everyday Life* (Harmony Books, 2017).

Sakyong Mipham, *Turning the Mind into an Ally* (Riverhead Books, 2003).

Helen Palmer, *The Enneagram: Understanding Yourself and the Others in Your Life* (HarperCollins, 1991).

Lodro Rinzler, *Love Hurts: Buddhist Advice for the Heartbroken* (Shambhala, 2016).

Shunryu Suzuki, *Zen Mind, Beginner's Mind: Informal Talks on Zen Meditation and Practice* (Shambhala, 2011).

Tulku Thondup, *The Heart of Unconditional Love: A Powerful New Approach to Loving-Kindness Meditation* (Shambhala, 2015).

Chögyam Trungpa, *Cutting through Spiritual Materialism* (Shambhala, 2008).

Chögyam Trungpa, *Shambhala: The Sacred Path of the Warrior* (Shambhala, 2003).

APPENDIX C

Questions

THESE ARE THE questions I received via Facebook when I mentioned I was working on this book and wondered what people might like to hear about. Thanks, FB posse!

Q. What should I do if my partner is unwilling to join me in this kind of relationship?

A. The most common question I hear is, "I'm willing to do these things, but my partner thinks it's all silly/irrational/pointless. What can I say to make him or her feel otherwise?"

The answer is nothing. There is nothing you can say to change someone else's point of view. In fact, attempting to do so is likely to result in further entrenchment, the very opposite of what you seek. So please don't do that absent a very clear opening and invitation.

There is only one way to convince someone that meditation, mindfulness, and these insights will make you more loving, brave, and strong and that is to show up to each interaction with love, bravery, and strength. In other words, don't say these things, *be* these things. There are no guarantees, but that is still the most compelling—and only—argument that cuts through.

Q. I parted with my former fiancé and father of my daughter because he could not stay sober and would not get the extensive help he needed. I hit my wall when I came home one evening to him blacked out on the couch after putting her to bed and then the next day having to leave my new job early to pick her up at school because he was too drunk to get her. I know I hit my official wall long after hitting weaker ones already along the way. I did not love him romantically unconditionally, which he demanded, and I question if that is really ever possible. We come from two different worlds when it comes to relationship expectations, demands, and promises, and romantic, family, friendship, or community relationships. I don't think relationships can withstand those differences. Thanks, and my apologies for the half rambling, half questioning.

A. Thanks for the great question, Sarah. It is not half rambling or half questioning. I think I understand what you are asking.

I do believe that unconditional love is possible—in moments. But it is unrealistic for anyone to think it is a state that one can arrive at never to depart. To demand it seems crazy, and in the way you describe it here, sounds less like a plea for love than one for tolerance or indulgence. As you will have seen in this book, I believe there are some things that are intolerable, including addiction and abuse. In such circumstances, it may be the case that the true expression of unconditional love is to stop trying to help.

When you hit the wall, you hit the wall. To argue that you have not hit the wall but are suffering from lack of lovingkindness is an obfuscation. First, no one but you knows where the wall is, how hard you've hit it, and how egregious the wounding is. Please remember: if there is any unconditional love to be expressed, its first recipient should be Sarah. This creates the ground for true compassion rather than a forced expression of some sort.

I can't help but wonder what this situation would be like if genders were reversed. Indulge me as I ponder stereotypes. If a man came home to find his woman passed out on the couch and upon awakening she tried to convince him that somehow this was his problem—is there any planet on which this would pass muster? I'm not saying it doesn't happen, I am hinting that women may be more socially conditioned to feel that if there is any problem, it is because *they* are not loving or kind enough. In response, I say: F*CK THAT. Please do what you feel is right and loving for yourself and your daughter. We are not here to be universal mommies.

Q. Dear Susan, I was wondering if the First Noble Truth could be understood as never really being satisfied in any relationship. I find myself being in relationships and always thinking the grass is greener on the other side. I go to the gym and see all these beautiful women and selfishly wonder if they would be more fun and sexy to be with. It's hard to admit this but it's true. I feel like a scumbag always looking at other women. I wonder how the Four Noble Truths could relate with this desire. I'm not sure if the desire is because I'm a perfectionist and think there is this perfect girlfriend out there, in which case is an impossible standard, or maybe there's something else to it. I'm not sure. Thanks for the question. Can't wait to hear from you and read your book.

A. What a great question. I truly appreciate the way you are attempting to blend your dharma study with seeing sexy women at the gym. Seriously! This is what it is all about—bringing your studies into your world and culture and making them relevant. Thank you.

I think you are right in your assessment of the First Noble Truth as having to do with an inability to feel satisfied. This does not mean that you should feel bad about yourself for experiencing this dissatisfaction. (It certainly does not mean you are a scumbag.)

As a student of the dharma, what is our first reaction to so-called negative emotion? I happen to know you and that you are a student of Buddhism—that is why I ask. If you said, "To make friends with it," I applaud you! Explore the feeling of dissatisfaction, but not the attendant storyline. In other words, what does it feel like to long for what you don't have because there may be something better out there? To get lost in the reasoning for your longing it is a detour. Study your state of mind and see where this leads instead.

Q. My daughter had been married for three months when her husband suffered a severe traumatic brain injury. His sweet personality, physical abilities, and cognitive abilities have changed, suddenly and drastically. She has dedicated herself to her "new Joshua" in the past two years since it happened, and this dedication is regularly renewed, as she, naturally, from time to time, questions what she's doing with the venerable "Should I stay or should I go?"

I'm happy to give you more background but the basic question remains the same. Her dedication is remarkable and her sense of humor is her saving grace! We give her support in any choice she makes, and love our son-in-law unconditionally.

A. I cannot imagine a more confusing, upsetting situation. I feel terrible for your daughter, and for your son-in-law. And you. There is clearly no obvious answer.

What I have to offer is not based in Buddhist wisdom but in the wisdom of Louise Piver, my own mother. When faced with complex decisions, her advice was to wait. "The really hard decisions make themselves," she always said to us.

At some point, causes and conditions will come together and your daughter will know what to do. She probably knows already—but knowing is not the same as doing. When the time is right, the path will be clear. Mom is right. Thanks, Mom! (Thank goodness for wise and caring moms.)

Q. How to wake up and see people and relationships clearly in the first six months of euphoria? What appears to be "not-suffering" leads to suffering later.

A. I love this question. It speaks to the strange shift from falling in love to being in love (or not) and the ensuing confusion. What happened to nonstop bliss? Staying in bed for days? Six-hour conversations? How is it possible to reconcile the way a relationship begins with what it turns into, a reckoning with all of our most wonderous *and* puniest qualities in a way that is by turns terrifying, compelling, beautiful, or stultifying?

As mentioned earlier, there is a difference between a love affair and a relationship. Not all love affairs make great relationships. Perhaps some of the suffering you allude to is about discovering that this person—the person you love to talk to, make love with, bask in the glow of—does not know how to hold a job, refuses to meet your family, or has a dark side that comes out when you disagree, qualities that would make a life together very difficult. There is great suffering when you find that the person you fell in love with does not exist, at least not in the way you imagined. Super painful, that.

However, I want to point out that the first six months of euphoria are not an illusion to be woken up from. I think such euphoria is real. It points to something. It means something. It is a time when you are shaken loose from your habitual views of self, other, and life, and is thus a moment of great possibility. To me, the question is not "How do I not do that?" but "What can I learn from what I am feeling right now?"

Hope this helps!

Q. When an intimate relationship has ended, run its course, how can it mature into another kind of love? And what about passion and jealousy?

A. Thanks for this question. I think you are asking about how to break up with someone and remain friends, minus any jealousy when one of you begins a new relationship. If this is the indeed the question, here is my answer:

You can't. Deep, intimate closeness in the context of a romantic relationship does not necessarily translate into another context. The relationship is over, that's it. You can't cherry-pick aspects of what you had ("We have such great conversations/are the only two people on earth who love puppet shows/still care about each other") and transplant them into a new relationship just because it seems like it should be possible. It almost never is. That is too conceptual.

Once you have had sex with someone, it is really, really difficult to back into a less intense relationship. Relationships don't seem able (or willing) to move backward. This doesn't mean you can't have a new relationship with this person, one of friendship, collegiality, fraternity, sisternity, whatever you like. But first the original relationship has to be completely over, meaning each party has released it and moved on. Then, perhaps, a new form of connection is possible.

Q. Does intimacy also allow us to discover how we're *not* connected to another?

A. Not sure if it does as a rule, per se, but there is certainly a great deal of loneliness in even the closest and most loving partnerships. It can happen that the more you love each other, the lonelier you feel because you eventually discover that there is a kind of unbridgeable gap between two people simply because you are two people. You find that there are ways your partner will never, ever be able to see you or understand you, not because they don't want to, but because they don't know how. That's just how it works. So I guess my answer is "yes."

Q. My question is/are: Does this wonderful feeling I am experiencing resonate truly and fully in my heart? Is there anything that doesn't feel right in my gut about this situation or person? What is it? How can I learn more while I love, accept, and honor myself through this process?

A. Dear Questioner, these are *the* questions. I am afraid that no one can answer them but you, however. A meditation practice can really help!

Q. Here is one I think about a lot: When you are doing your best to bring Buddhist teachings to the interactions in your relationship but your partner is not (a non-Buddhist), how do you keep from feeling like you take on the burden of the communication and stability in the relationship? On the flip side of that, how do you keep from being a total a**hole when you are really feeling the pinch of being the one moving the communication and interactions forward? I would love more discussion on finding balance between personal practice and living a committed relationship with someone who has no interest in Buddhism.

A. For my thoughts on being in a relationship when one person is a practitioner and the other is not, please see chapter 2. See also Question #1.

Further, I would say that the onus of taking responsibility for communication, stability, and balance has nothing to do with whether or not you are a Buddhist. I know plenty of recalcitrant, nutty, unbalanced Buddhists. We have no special claim on decency, goodness, and emotional maturity.

For myself, I enjoy being in a relationship with a non-Buddhist because I can't hide behind what I like to call "Buddhist bullsh*t." I can't consign blame for our problems to his lack of spiritual insight versus my superior knowing. If only! We are both just human beings here, and while a meditation practice is of great importance when it comes to love (indeed, this entire book is about just that), there is no substitute for emotional skillfulness and openhearted bravery, neither of which we Buddhists have a special claim to. If your partner is unwilling or unable to communicate well or contribute to building a steady relationship, I warrant it has nothing to do with spiritual practice but is about something else.

Q. Someone asked me for advice about this last night—what do you do when you are getting to know someone and they do something that is difficult to deal with—repeatedly—it is part of who they are. If you decide to stay in the relationship, how do you deal with it? How do you know if it is a deal breaker?

A. Wish I could have heard your answer!

The person you are in a relationship with is eventually going to do something that is difficult to deal with. Repeatedly. It depends on what it is and what your values are. If the person turns out to be cruel in any way whatsoever, I would say RED ALERT. The same goes for issues related to addiction.

It is very, very difficult when your partner is awesome, say, 97 percent of the time, and truly horrible (or worse) in the other 3 percent. To know what to do requires way more than I or anyone else could say from this remote distance. There is no substitute for counseling and expert advice meant for the individual personally.

Aside from abuse and addiction, there are plenty of other issues that could be deal breakers such as if religious observation is a core value for one while for the other it is not. It differs from couple to couple and, in all cases, it is really important to know what the deal breakers are for each.

Q. What is love and how do you know when it is real?—KW (16 years old)

A. KW, in five to ten years, you are going to have to tell me. In the meantime, all I can say is that you can totally trust yourself to know, if not on the spot, then eventually. Please believe that about yourself.

Q. Given that the only constant in this universe is change, how do you manage the trials of the dynamic nature of love as it changes face throughout a long term relationship?

A. Exactly! That is 100 percent what this book is about. I truly hope you have found it useful. Do let me know.

Q. How do you deal with the resentment after a breakup?

A. First, my heart goes out to you if you are dealing with a broken heart. That is truly one of the most searingly painful experiences a person can go through. I wrote a whole 'nother book about this, *The Wisdom of a Broken Heart*. I also recommend my good friend Lodro Rinzler's book, *Love Hurts*. Both are based in the Buddhist tradition and are about working with the loss of romantic love.

In the meantime, my best advice is to be very gentle with yourself. Of course you feel resentment. (And probably many other things, too.) Allow yourself to feel it all. As much as you are able to, please try to let go of the storyline that accompanies what you feel to just *feel*. To "feel the feeling and drop the story," as Pema Chödron has counseled, is truly the royal road to release. For more on this, you could read her book, *The Places That Scare You*. Highly recommended.

AFTERWORD

DUNCAN AND I each got home from work later than usual last night. I had been consumed with computer problems of the most frustrating sort and had spent hours on the phone with tech support instead of working on this very book, which, at the time of this writing, is due in about ten days. I was exhausted, frustrated, feeling pressured—and my computer still wasn't working.

Duncan was late because his place of employment is suddenly undergoing tumultuous change and he, as one of the leaders of the company, is deeply enmeshed in it.

By the time I walked in the door, he was already in bed reading. I sat down on the bed next to him, still in my coat because it has been one of those winters here in New England—days on end of single-digit temperatures. "How was your day?" I asked. "Massive," he said. My breath caught in my chest. This, from someone who would describe a broken bone as "irritating" and a 100 percent raise as "nice." Not given to hyperbole, my husband. He had all my attention.

He showed me an email that had been sent around his place of employment describing game-changing org chart shifts, leaving him and other colleagues with much greater responsibilities in the company.

My reaction was twofold: delight and pride at his accomplishment and deep, inexpressible dismay. Why the latter? Because for more than fifteen years we have lived in a place I dislike. No offense, Boston. I know a lot of people love you, but for me you are not home and my life partner had just accepted a new role at his company that would tie us here even more tightly. I could feel the walls closing in on me. My breath shortened. Would I never find a home that felt like home? I felt so trapped, but after our mutually exhausting, frustrating, game-changing (for him), freezing cold days, it was not the time to take it up.

We went to sleep, not touching each other. In the middle of the night, I woke up with a migraine, which is an all-too-common experience in my life. If you have a problem with headaches, you may know that, just like rain storms, some are more epic than others. I could immediately tell that this was one such headache. I got up and took my migraine medication, but when I woke up a few hours later at 6:00 a.m., I still had the pain. *Oh no.* This was the kind that could land me in the emergency room. I got out of bed anyway and went to my office (which is in the apartment next door to ours) and saw that my computer was *still* restoring itself and that there were six more hours to go. When would I get to my writing? I sat on the couch and began to stew. I was stuck. Stuck in Boston. Stuck with chronic migraines. Stuck with a dead computer. Stuck in the cold. Stuck trying to finish this book.

Duncan would never understand me, I realized. He would never see how big of an issue this—home—was in my life and how difficult it had been for me to put my dissatisfaction aside every single day. *For fifteen years.* Didn't he know that someday I would reach a breaking point? Come to think of it, that breaking point was here. It was happening *right now. Okay*, I thought, *I'm on my own here. No one is going to help me. I'm going to have to take matters into my own hands*. (This, by the way, has been my shadow mindset since childhood.) *I will figure out a way to move by myself. If it means our relationship is over, so be it. He is losing me. He doesn't even realize it.* I felt coldness in my veins.

I went back to our house to get my coat because when headaches get this bad, it often helps to take a walk. Even though it was 19 degrees Fahrenheit out, I had to do it. I knew he was still getting ready for work, but I hoped I could get in and out without too much interaction.

I could already feel myself separating from him.

Then I saw him at the top of the stairs in his boxers and T-shirt, about to get in the shower, but he stopped and beckoned to me. I walked up to him. He knew that tipping my head back would hurt, so he stood one step below me and held out his arms. I stepped into his embrace and as I did, I felt my heart begin to melt a little. Maybe he did love me and care about me after all. We held each other for a few sweet moments. "How are you this morning?" he asked. I mentioned the headache. I took a beat. Should I tell him about my reactions to his workplace changes? *Fuck it*, I thought. *Yes, I will.* "And I feel like we're never going to move. It's killing me." In response, he dropped his arms and jerked his head away from me in frustration. This issue again? *Again*?

I was stung. I turned on him and headed back down the stairs. "This is not good," I said, meaning that his response was really, really upsetting to me and had just made a quantum shift in the distance between us. Whatever had begun to thaw froze again. He watched me walk away. "I can't do anything right," he said.

I snatched my coat off its hook and ran to the door. *I have to get out of here, I have to get out of here, I have to get out of here.* I was outraged at being ignored, discounted, rejected—until the moment I bent down to put on my boots, when anger turned on a dime into extraordinary and unbearable sorrow. I started to cry. And cry. And *cry*. I dropped my keys on the ground, crouched down on the floor in my coat, barefoot, held my head in my hands, and shook. He was at the opposite end of the house and would not be able to hear me so I let go into the sobbing. Tears led to more tears, and when I thought I had reached the end of a sobbing cycle, I discovered another uncried well. *I feel so lonely. It's over. It's over. It's over*, I thought.

Then I felt a hand on my shoulder. It was him, still in boxers and T-shirt, and he pulled me to him. He lay down on the carpet with me in his arms. I cried for a long time. I felt the warmth of his flesh and tightened my arms about his neck. "Shhh, shhh," he whispered. "I can't change our living situation," I said. "I can't change my headaches. I can't finish my book." "I know," he said. "I love you." "I love you, too," I said. We lay there breathing together and I thought about how we just had passed through every phase of a relationship. "It's not even seven a.m. yet," I said and we laughed.

Up. Down. Close. Distant. Connected. Disconnected. Repeat, repeat, repeat. Conditions are constantly shifting, but your heart is always as clear and open as the sky. When you trust your own heart, you can allow the entire scope of experience to touch you. This is the mark of the spiritual warrior. She can hold sweetness, sorrow, rage, and delight equally and fully. She can watch as emotions rise and fall, notice how she reaches out to some and recoils from others, and know that somehow she'll find a way to make whatever she experiences a part of love's path. Whether her world is friendly or inhospitable, smooth or rocky, she can abide in it wholeheartedly. A loving heart is as infinite as the sky and, like the sky, can contain sunshine and storms, snowflakes and hail. Whatever passes through, the sky is always the sky. It never gives up. From within it, the great sun rises in the east, the moon meets the tide, and the circle is always complete.

ACKNOWLEDGMENTS

DEAR READER, IF you felt what I am feeling as I write these notes of thanks, you would be most impressed by the level of gratitude I'm trying to express even as I know I will fail.

Gratitude has always struck me as one of the most complex emotional states. It is a path in and of itself, at once filled with appreciation and contorted with frustration. I am SO APPRECIATIVE, and there is no one to give back to! No matter how much I thank people, no matter how eloquently and specifically I name what others have done for me and why it has changed my life, and no matter what I try to do to repay them—I simply cannot. They just look at me and shrug. "Oh, okay. Whatevs. You're welcome." Like it's no big deal. It is so exasperating. I've come to see that gratitude is a one-way street between recipient and giver. The only way to honor the debt is to give what they have given me to someone else. In this sense, this book was written for them.

Gratitude first and always to my guides along the dharmic path: to Chögyam Trungpa Rinpoche, who pointed me home; to Sakyong Mipham Rinpoche for explaining how to get there; and to Tulku Thondup Rinpoche for allowing me to sit on his couch while he somehow alters my mindstream by his presence.

Sam Bercholz has been my friend, my brother, my heart's companion since even before the journey began and I thank him for showing me in a thousand ways what really matters. My dear Sam, you have given me courage. I can repay you only by achieving complete enlightenment. Way to set the bar.

My dharma sister and treasured friend Crystal Gandrud not only encouraged me as I wrote, she shared my view and was my creative companion as this book took shape. Just knowing that she was going to read it forced me to up my game because of the respect I have for her brilliance, discernment, and inner richness. Thank you for visiting us from Planet Genius, Crystal. Give all the other geniuses our best regards.

I thank that other visitor from Planet Genius, Seth Godin, for being a tirelessly generous friend with the unique ability to encourage and challenge me equally. (How do you do that?!) Your heart is as big as the world. Thank you for teaching us all how to build a bridge between the world of meaning and the world of commerce in a way that honors both. (How do you do that?!) I am always your friend.

My beloved friend and colleague Jenna Hollenstein is the cheering section every writer dreams of. Thank you for wanting this book to be written and for encouraging me to think that I could do it—and for demonstrating what capaciousness actually looks like. You amaze me and I am your friend for life.

Michele Gare and Lisa Fehl held down the fort at the Open Heart Project with such care and commitment that I felt free to write this book, knowing that our community was being taken care of with love and respect. Thank you, thank you.

Thank you to the world's best dharma IM posse—Crystal, Emily Bower, Greg Pierotti, and Kevin Townley—for your unceasing interest in exactly what interests me most. Thank you for being so smart, funny, and real. Thank you for the threads of sanity.

I thank my brother Christopher Kilmer for his outer, inner, and secret efforts to make the entire world secure, especially for his closest friends. I feel your protection. You are Kasung.

And to my other Kasung brother, Michael Carroll, for his deep insight, fearless devotion, and epic friendship. You have taught me so much. You are an emissary from the crazy-wisdom world of sanity and I love you.

I'm grateful to my comrades-in-arms Jonathan Fields and Charlie Gilkey for sharing their brilliance on a regular basis. You are important companions on the journey to build a life where work, love, and creativity are not separate.

I thank my girl Jen Louden for sneaking away with me to write and for being relentlessly encouraging, genuine, and inspiring. And funny! And beautiful! I love you!

I thank my girl Christine Kane for sharing soulful wisdom, truth, and tacos and for demonstrating how to achieve what you want by being exactly who you are. I love you!

I thank my friend, the lion-hearted Joel Marcus, for his intense devotion to love and truth. You are absolutely fearless and I love you.

Many thanks to our new colleagues at Page Two Strategies for their support, and expertise, and for being true "book people."

I also thank the following for their friendship and inspiration. Each of you influenced the writing of this book, whether you know it or not: Josh Baran, Duncan Browne IV, Robert Chender, Colleen Lutz Clemens, Beth Grossman, Ishita Gupta, Gayle Hanson, Kaleigh Isaacs, Pico Iyer, Ming and Kate Linsley (and Auds and Slatercakes), Melvin McLeod, Derek O'Brien, Lodro Rinzler, Chalo Smukler, Rod Meade Sperry, Ryan Stagg, Michael Bungay Stanier, Stephanie Tade, John Tarrant, Roshi, and Martha Winthrop.

My companions as I wrote this book were John Coltrane and Johnny Hartman. Listening to them compels one to reach higher.

For my family: my loving and devoted mother, Louise; adventurous and hilarious brother, David (and the wonderful Julie); brilliant and rock-solid sister, Carol, who is also my twin (and that Ed); nephew Forrest, niece Allison, and step-niece Lisa. I thank my in-law siblings Louisa and Eliot Vestner, Bette and John Cooper, and Tom and Maricel Browne. Thank you for loving me and each other and for showing me what commitment to family looks like.

I thank my late father, Julius Piver, M.D., J.D., for having been a walking, talking heart of love and tenderness.

Dad, my earliest memories are of your gentleness. Your kindness runs in my veins.

Finally, I express inexpressible gratitude to my partner, friend, husband, and heart's closest companion, Duncan Browne. Every time you asked me what I was writing about and I said *you*, you laughed. Uh oh. Now you know I was not joking. Thank you for making space for me in your heart. Thank you for always being willing to love me more. Thank you for making a home for and with me. Thank you for holding on loosely but never letting go.

ABOUT THE AUTHOR

SUSAN PIVER is the *New York Times* best-selling author of nine books, including *The Hard Questions*, the award-winning *How Not to Be Afraid of Your Own Life*, *The Wisdom of a Broken Heart*, and *Start Here Now: An Open-Hearted Guide to the Path and Practice of Meditation*.

Susan has an international reputation for being an exceptionally skillful meditation teacher. She teaches workshops and speaks on mindfulness, resilience, communication, relationships, and creativity. She has been a student of Buddhism since 1995, graduated from a Buddhist seminary in 2004, and was authorized to teach meditation in the Shambhala Buddhist lineage in 2005.

In 2012, she created the Open Heart Project, a virtual mindfulness community with more than twenty thousand members all over the world.

For more information, free downloads, and support for working with the themes of this book, please visit **susanpiver.com/4ntl-resources.**